Medieval London

Kenneth Derwent

SBN 356 02480 6
Macdonald & Co. (Publishers) Ltd.
First published in 1968 by
Macdonald & Co. (Publishers) Ltd.
St. Giles House, 49 Poland Street, London W.1
Reprinted 1969

Made and printed in Great Britain by
Purnell & Sons Ltd., Paulton, Somerset

Discovering London 3
Medieval London
Kenneth Derwent

MACDONALD : LONDON

Contents

Cover: a detail from the Luttrell Psalter showing the murder of Thomas Becket (British Museum)

Slip case illustration: Visscher's Panorama of London 1616 (Guildhall Museum)
Drawings by David Newton

London in the Middle Ages

This book, the third in the 'Discovering London' series, covers the period between the accession of King John in 1199, and the death of Richard III in 1485.

Many people imagine that there was little change during this period in the way that people lived; but we should remember that for somebody living in the reign of Richard III, King John seems about as far away as Charles II does to us! This long period was just as eventful as were the last three hundred years and witnessed many important developments in English society.

At the start of the book, England is seen as a divided country with a small Norman-French ruling class keeping the Anglo-Saxon population firmly in its place; by the end, England is a nation in her own right. Although she is still recovering from the Wars of the Roses, the long struggle for the throne, her people now feel that they really are English. The country has a powerful middle class of merchants and traders, the beginnings of a parliament, and is poised on the brink of the great overseas expansion which was to reach its climax in the reign of Queen Elizabeth I.

Throughout this period, London maintained and increased its position as the most important city in the country. In 1132 Henry I granted the City a charter, recognising the county status of the City, the authority of

5

its local courts, and its right, unmatched anywhere else in England, to elect its own sheriffs. The first mayor, Henry FitzAylwin, had been elected in 1191 or 1192; and although King John insisted that the mayor-elect should be approved by him or his Justiciar, Magna Carta recognised the importance of the City by naming the Mayor of London among those appointed to ensure that the terms of the Great Charter were carried out. The cynics say that London gave its support to the barons in exchange for this clause in the Charter, but the City was always eager to acquire new rights and status and was prepared to accept extra obligations in order to get them.

London's geographical position, which led to its creation in the first place, ensured its survival as the most important, largest, and wealthiest city and port in England. Much play is made these days of the fact that modern London pays about one sixth of England's Schedule 'D' income tax; but 'twas ever thus—when the Danish king Canute imposed a tribute on the country in the early 11th century, London paid one seventh of it!

The Middle Ages, then, saw increasing prosperity for London, great growth in its trade with Europe, and the emergence of its merchants as supporters—or, on occasion, opponents—of the Crown, of such importance that they could not be ignored. The wealth of the city or of its individual citizens was frequently at the disposal of the king, either voluntarily or by compulsion; but we may be sure that the Londoners seldom parted with their money, even when it was extorted, without some compensation in the way of status or privileges.

The city had its ups and downs, of course. In the 13th century Henry III refused to accept the mayor-elect, one Thomas FitzThomas, whereupon London transferred its support to Simon de Montfort in his rebellion against the king. Henry was defeated by the rebel forces, his power was very much curtailed, and he had perforce to accept FitzThomas, who swore allegiance to the king

6

Simon de Montfort's official seal

provided he treated the City well! By 1341, however, crown and city were on good terms again, and Edward III gave London the right to amend its own constitution.

Since London was so closely concerned with the history of England in general, a short summary of events in each reign has been included (see page 72) so that readers can understand the background against which the city grew and the forces which shaped the lives of its citizens. The rest is directly concerned with the city—its architecture, its government, the livery companies, and some famous people and events of the period. At the end of the book are some suggestions for walks to guide you round what remains of medieval London.

The Buildings of Medieval London

In the Middle Ages many important and well-established towns were really little more than large villages. There were probably no more than four or five cities in England with more than a thousand houses each, notably York, Norwich, Bristol, and Coventry.

One indication of how important a town was in the Middle Ages is the number of medieval churches it contains. You will find that the four cities named above all have several (York still has about a dozen). On the other hand, in towns of comparatively recent development you will find only one—the original parish church of the village. Examples of this are Birmingham and Bradford.

The fact that medieval London had *over one hundred* churches is a measure of the outstanding importance of the city in those times. Yet by modern standards it was quite a small place, containing perhaps 50,000 people.

Lesser town houses

Apart from the favoured few—royalty, noblemen, bishops, and some increasingly prosperous merchants, with whom we shall deal later—the Londoners lived in squalor. The streets were very narrow and the houses were in the same style and of the same materials as were used for country cottages in south-east England, timber, plaster, and thatch. Londoners, like other Englishmen, used the building materials which were most readily

8

available. Wood, usually oak from the Sussex Weald, was used for the frames of houses, the spaces in between being filled in with split wattles interwoven and coated with clay or some sort of plaster. Later, bricks might be used for the in-filling—a practice introduced from the Netherlands. This type of building was of course far less durable than stone and this fact, coupled with the frequent outbreaks of fire, has ensured that no medieval wooden houses have survived in London.

It is an interesting fact that by the beginning of the 16th century 'pre-fabs' had been invented. There are records in Guildhall of four three-storey houses built in Rood Lane in 1505, the timber frames of which were made at Maldon in Essex and sent to London ready for erection. This seems to have been fairly common practice. I heard recently of beams from a derelict medieval cottage being transported a considerable distance for use in restoring another cottage; it was found that the substitute timbers fitted perfectly into place, even the holes for the securing pegs tallying with those in the beams of the cottage being restored.

Here is a list of timber-framed buildings still visible in London. They are *not* medieval, since they date from the 16th and early 17th centuries, but they are in the style and tradition of the Middle Ages:

Staple Inn, Holborn. Late 16th century; formerly connected with the wool trade.

The Old Curiosity Shop, Portsmouth Street. Just off Kingsway, by Lincolns Inn Fields. Built in 1567 and originally two tiny shops.

Gatehouse of St. Bartholomew-the-Great, West Smithfield. 16th century. Built over an archway which was formerly the south-west door of the church. The nave was pulled down after the Dissolution and the site is now the churchyard. The timberwork of the house was plastered over at some subsequent date, and forgotten. It took bombs dropped from a Zeppelin in the Great War

9

to shake the plaster off and reveal the original form of the house.

Prince Henry's Room, Fleet Street. Early 17th century. Believed to have been the council chamber of the Duchy of Cornwall. Prince Henry, eldest son of James I, was (as the Prince of Wales always is) Duke of Cornwall.

Why the Overhang?

Why do the upper storeys of timbered buildings project beyond the lower floors? It is merely a matter of mechanics. If you built a wooden-framed house with straight-up walls the weight of the inmates and furniture would make the upper floors sag, like this:

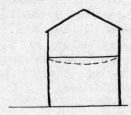

But if you made it like this, the weight of the upper walls and roof would counterbalance that of the contents:

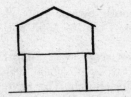

—and this could be repeated, within reason, for three, four, or even five floors. Hence the overhang you see in medieval and early Tudor buildings.

Growth of the Merchant's House

Records of the 13th century mention fifteen shop-fronts in the space of 150 feet in the Cheapside area. As the tradesman, with his family and apprentices, lived over the shop and usually made and stored his wares on the premises, conditions must have been unbelievably cramped. 'Journeymen' and other hired labourers usually lived in tenements known as rents. In Westminster there is a narrow turning off Great Peter Street which preserves such a name—Perkins Rents.

As the medieval merchants grew wealthier, the houses they built in London came to resemble those of the nobility more closely. The hall rose to the full height of the two-storeyed house, and behind would be a store for the merchant's goods with a private family room above it known as a 'solar'. The kitchen, pantry, dairy, and other domestic spaces would be separated from the house, partly as a fire precaution. Throughout the later Middle Ages more private rooms would be added, with fireplaces built into the walls and glass in the windows instead of horn. The staircase to the upper rooms would now be indoors instead of against the outside wall. The roof would be tiled, or sometimes of lead. There might even be a small garden. But in most cases the merchant would still carry on his trade from the house, as well as in the market. Here is an extract from the articles of the Cordwainers' Company as proposed in a petition to the Mayor in 1375:

. . . That no one shall expose his wares openly for sale in market on Sundays at any place, but only within his own dwelling to serve the common people . . .

By the 15th century some citizens of London could almost be called merchant princes, so great was their wealth and so splendid the state in which they lived. They were of course mostly traders, not craftsmen, exporting English wool and importing all manner of costly

and rare goods from Europe and the East. One such was
Sir John Crosby, who in 1466 built himself a mansion in
Bishopsgate. The house seems to have been used quite
often by royalty, foreign ambassadors, and so on, perhaps
lent to them (or rented?) by Sir John. The mansion was
pulled down about 1908 but its great hall was dismantled
and rebuilt on Chelsea Embankment, close to Chelsea
Old Church, where it can still be seen. It is now part of a
residence for women post-graduate students and can be
visited (see Appendix A).

*Elevation and plan of a manor house. Although these were
still designed for defence, there was a growing demand for
greater comfort and improved living conditions.*

Decay of the Great Hall

During the later Middle Ages the trend away from the communal life of family, retainers, servants, and guests in the great hall and towards more privacy, at least for the family, continued. By the time Crosby built his mansion the process was almost complete, and from then on the hall was used only for ceremonial purposes and grand occasions. The earlier communal life now exists only in institutions such as schools and colleges. Evidence of it can best be seen in the halls of the Oxford and Cambridge colleges, many of which survive almost unaltered from the Middle Ages or a little later. Most of them can be visited when not in use; times vary, so please ask at the porter's lodge of the college.

Episcopal Palaces

In such a 'built-up area' as medieval London there obviously was little scope for the building of great palaces with the extensive gardens and grounds considered appropriate to prelates. Consequently most of them were built outside the city walls, as were the monastic houses. Although almost all of them have now disappeared—the Archbishop of Canterbury's palace at Lambeth is an exception—there is still evidence of their existence. Close to Southwark Cathedral is a narrow street called Winchester Walk, and the riverside warehouses nearby cover the site of the palace of the bishops of Winchester. Just off Holborn Circus there is a short street named Ely Place which occupies the site of the medieval palace of the bishops of that See.

Royal Palaces

For royal palaces and for noblemen's and bishops' houses, the Gothic style described in the article on church architecture was used. There are very few survivals to be seen in London.

Westminster Hall

From at least the reign of Edward the Confessor there has been a royal palace near the Abbey, and the official name of the Houses of Parliament is still the Palace of Westminster. This great hall was originally erected by William Rufus, son of the Conqueror, about 1090, but was buttressed, re-roofed, and altered by Richard II three hundred years later. The hammerbeam roof of the hall, made up of two tiers of timber half-arches jutting inward from the walls, is famous; it has an unsupported span of 67 feet and is the largest of its type in the world.

Here the king and his family, with the noblemen, officials, and retainers of the court, would eat their meals together and enjoy their dancing and other festivities on special occasions. It was also the setting for more formal gatherings, such as a coronation banquet, when the King's Champion would ride in among the hundreds of guests, fully armed, fling down his gauntlet, and challenge to single combat anyone who questioned the king's right to the throne.

The hall also became the centre of administration of the king's justice when it was decided that the chief judges should no longer travel the country in the wake of the court (which was always on the move) but remain static at Westminster, where litigants could always find them. The Court of King's Bench and the other divisions of the High Court were here until the building of the Royal Courts of Justice in the Strand in the late 19th century, and many famous trials were held here, among them those of William Wallace, Anne Boleyn, and King Charles I.

In its days as the great hall of the palace the flight of steps at the south end did not exist. Instead there was a low dais on which the high table for the king, his immediate family, and favoured courtiers was set. The re-

14

mainder of the company would sit at long tables ranged down the length of the hall. In the middle there was a large stone fire-hearth, and in the timber roof above it a louvre or hole to let out the smoke. The pinnacle you can see from outside on the roof of the hall now covers this primitive chimney-hole.

The Jewel Tower

Just across the road from the Victoria Tower of the Houses of Parliament, this little tower is, like West-minster Hall, a survivor of the fire which destroyed the old palace in 1834. The Jewel Tower was built in 1365/6, when the hall was being rebuilt, and was used for some time as the treasury for the crown jewels, and later as the repository for the official archives of parliament.

Eltham Palace

The manor of Eltham first came into royal hands on the death of Anthony Bek, Bishop of Durham, in 1311. It was a favourite residence of Edward II and his son Edward III, and was greatly enlarged and improved by them. When complete, the palace was probably almost the size of Hampton Court. The moat enclosed an area of 340 feet by 300 feet, and additional courts brought the total up to about 1,000 feet by 400 feet, as far as can now be judged. King Henry VI built a new great hall for the palace, but his rival and successor Edward IV pulled it down and replaced it with the one still standing. It has a fine hammerbeam roof and can be visited.

How to Get There

Details of opening times and routes to all the above are in Appendix A.

Church Architecture in the Middle Ages

Five Styles

The Middle Ages are contemporary with the development of church architecture from Norman to Perpendicular Gothic. Here is a brief description of the differences between these styles and the ones which flourished in between.

The **Norman** style, identified mainly by its round-topped arches, is known on the Continent as Romanesque. It was introduced into England before the Norman Conquest and was in vogue until about the middle of the 12th century. Then came a short **Transitional** period, and then Gothic.

The **Gothic** style, distinguished by pointed arches, was in use for over four hundred years and was then displaced by the revived classical or Renaissance style. Gothic is divided into three periods, each lasting about one hundred to a hundred and fifty years, but overlapping each other and changing gradually all the time. We call these three phases **Early English**, **Decorated**, and **Perpendicular**. In the first the arches are tall, simple, and narrow, the 'lancet' type. In the middle or Decorated period the windows become broader and the stone tracery of their mullions first assumed geometrical patterns, and later rushed into elaborate curly designs of great exuberance. This style in turn gave way to the third and last phase of Gothic, the Perpendicular, in which the emphasis is mainly on vertical line. During the four centuries of Gothic architecture the pillars gradually changed from solid, plain piers to clusters of slender shafts rising straight up from the pavement of the church without a break to the vaulting or ceiling, and there spreading out into lovely splayed ribs known as fan vaulting. This was an exclusively English development.

Norman Inflexibility

The Norman style suffered from one great limitation, its inflexibility. You see, if you use a semi-circular arch its height is directly related to the distance between the pillars it rests on—the closer the pillars the lower the arch. Like this :

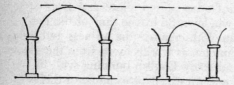

So if for any reason you wanted to place the pillars closer together, and yet maintain the same height of arch, the narrower arch had to be put on 'stilts' to bring it up to the same height as the broader one. Thus :

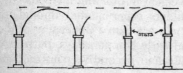

which is not really very elegant. You can see an example of this in the arcade of the ambulatory round the choir of St. Bartholomew-the-Great at Smithfield.

The invention of the pointed Gothic arch changed this at a stroke. From now on it didn't matter how much you varied the distance between the pillars; you could still maintain an equal height of arch throughout your building:

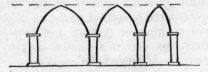

Buttresses and Windows

Another important development during the Middle Ages was the discovery by church builders that by buttressing the walls on the outside they could be relieved of much of the weight and outward thrust of the stone vaulting overhead. With less weight for the walls to carry, the windows could be made bigger. As this process continued during the Gothic period, more and more space was given to the windows. So by the time of the Perpendicular period (late 15th century) the airiness and lightness inside the church was worlds away from the gloom of the Norman and Early English building with its narrow slits of windows. An excellent example of this is the nave of St. George's Chapel at Windsor, where almost all the wall space between the buttresses is occupied by glass.

The development of the buttress illustrates the continual striving for improvement in building methods with which the inventive builders experimented throughout the Middle Ages. From no more than a thickening of the wall, as in the Saxon and early Norman days, buttresses evolved into the elaborate and decorative constructions of the 15th century.

An additional refinement (which seems to have been introduced on the Continent much earlier than in England) was the flying buttress. This brilliant innovation enabled the builders to carry the thrust of the vaulting over a projecting lower portion of the building such as a side aisle, and so to a buttress firmly anchored in the ground beyond. It was in fact a half-arch spanning the gap between the main wall and the buttress:

Westminster Abbey has some splendid flying buttresses, especially on the south side, where the thrust is carried over the south aisle of the nave *and* the north walk of the cloister. They are best seen from Dean's Yard.

There are very many other examples of flying buttresses. Some very fancy ones dating from about 1500 (late Perpendicular) can be seen around the Henry VII Chapel at Westminster.

Rude Word

The term 'Gothic' was first applied to the medieval style in a sneering, derogatory sort of way by the exponents of the neo-classical or Renaissance style which displaced it in the late 16th century. It has nothing to do with the Goths, who would not have recognised a church had they seen one.

Examples in or near London

Norman (1050–1150)	Chapel of St. John, Tower of London.
	St. Bartholomew-the-Great, Smithfield.
	Crypt of St. Mary-le-Bow, Cheapside.
	Waltham Abbey, Essex.

Early English (1150–1300)	Westminster Abbey.
	Choir of Southwark cathedral.
	Chancel of Temple church.
	Part of St. Helen's church, Bishopsgate.
Decorated (1270–1400)	Church at Stone, near Dartford.
	Church of St. Etheldreda, Ely Place, Holborn.
	St. Stephen's Crypt, Houses of Parliament.
Perpendicular (1350–1550)	Henry VII Chapel, Westminster Abbey.
	St. Margaret, Westminster.
	Eton College chapel.
	St. George's chapel, Windsor.

How to Get There

See Appendix A.

A contemporary drawing of builders at work

London Bridge

Although rivers were extensively used for the transport of passengers and goods in the Middle Ages, it is not generally realised what an obstacle they were to travellers whose routes did not coincide with the direction of the waterways. Fords could be dangerous, especially when rivers were in spate, and ferry crossings too were sometimes hazardous; but bridges were few and far between and often entailed long detours. So bridges and towns benefited each other; the bridge attracted trade to the town and the town offered accommodation to the traveller and provided funds for the upkeep of the bridge.

It is known that there was a bridge across the Thames at London in the Roman days. Indeed, the fact that this, the upper limit of tidal water then, was the lowest point at which the river could be bridged was one of the reasons for the city being here. The bridge undoubtedly fell into disrepair in the centuries following the Roman withdrawal, and no record has survived of any rebuilding which might have taken place, but we know that a bridge existed in the 10th and 11th centuries.

Between 1176 and 1209 a new bridge was built, this time of stone instead of wood, with nineteen arches, and

A typical medieval seal used for witnessing documents

stout piers protected from passing craft by boat-shaped wooden piling known as 'starlings'. Later, houses and shops were built on the bridge and a chapel dedicated to St. Thomas Becket (a Londoner, by the way) was added where travellers could say a prayer for their safe passage and—it was hoped—leave a donation towards the up-keep of the bridge. A drawbridge and a fortified gate-house were built to secure the southern end of the bridge, and it became the custom to exhibit here the heads of traitors executed on Tower Hill and elsewhere.

The cost of maintenance was very heavy, since damage to the bridge and especially to the starlings was frequent.

The narrow arches contributed to this, for at certain states of the tide they caused a difference in water level above and below the bridge of 6 feet, with the consequence that the river poured through the arches like a millrace and exerted great pressure. Rents paid for the shops and houses on the bridge were put towards this expense, and these were augmented by legacies and donations of money and property from public-spirited citizens and fraternities. These funds are now consolidated into a trust under the control of the Bridge House Estates Committee of the Corporation and produce an annual income of about £750,000. All four bridges owned by the City—London, Blackfriars, Southwark, and Tower Bridges—are financed from these funds.

The medieval bridge lasted until 1831 when it was pulled down and replaced by the present one. In late 1968 work began on yet another London Bridge on the same site. The £3-4,000,000 cost of this will be met out of the Bridge House Estates funds, and no charge will fall on the ratepayer.

Living Conditions

Indoors

In its simplest form the medieval Londoner's house was a squalid, unhealthy hovel. Built of timber and clay, as we have seen, it would probably have no more than two rooms. The floor would be of beaten earth, perhaps strewn with rushes. In winter it would be cold, damp and smelly; in summer hot and smelly. If it had a fire at all, it would be in a clay-lined depression or on a slab of stone in the floor, the smoke having to escape as best it could through the thatch. The 'windows' would be small and unglazed, and in cold weather they would be closed by wooden shutters, cutting down the already limited light to almost total darkness. After sunset the only lighting would be by tallow candles (cheaper than wax) or more probably by tallow dip—smoky, dim and evil-smelling. If the house had more than one floor the stair would be an external ladder.

Sanitary arrangements were primitive and consisted at most of a rudimentary earth closet; but many of the citizens had to use the public latrines provided in each ward. Such animals as the householder might own would share the 'comforts' of the home with the family.

The furniture would hardly compete with what a modern camper—and a stoic at that—would consider the absolute minimum; a trestle table, a wooden bench, a couple of stools, the beds mere ledges with straw-filled palliasses. One can imagine with what joy the medieval family would welcome the end of winter and the approach of spring, with the prospect of escape from these miserable surroundings into the fresh air!

In the better-class town houses one might find wooden floors and in the wealthiest even stone paving or tiles. Furniture would include a few wooden chairs and stools, and probably big chests both for seating and for storing household goods. Rushes would still be strewn on the floor, unless the owner were able to afford an imported rug or two. The wooden bed-frames would have a criss-cross mesh of rope netting to support the feather mattresses, and for the richer a four-poster canopy with hangings would help to keep out the injurious night air after bedtime.

In the poorer houses wooden platters and bowls would be used at table, with the minimum of cutlery—the normal eating implements in most homes were knives and fingers. The middle-class Londoner would use pewter plates and mugs, and perhaps a spoon made of cow's horn. His wife might also be the proud possessor of a piece or two of glazed earthenware—but one imagines this would be kept 'for best'. There are some examples of green glaze and of brown and yellow slipware in the Guildhall Museum.

The top-class merchant would probably have provided his house with tapestries or some form of fabric wall-hangings. There might be down-filled cushions on the wooden chairs and rugs on the floor—perhaps even a skin or two if he had a friend in the fur trade. There would be plenty of good wax candles in sconces or lanterns. If his wife still scattered rushes as a floor-covering, she would mix some sweet-smelling herbs among them.

If the house were suitably placed, for instance backing on to the Walbrook, it might have a privy or latrine discharging straight into the stream—a very refined adjunct not enjoyed by many citizens.

Even such sophisticated furnishings as these, however, would not spell comfort to us; no interior-sprung mattresses, no upholstered armchairs, no electric light or gas fires, no washing-up liquid 'kind to your hands', no running water, and no draught-excluders!

The Streets

The streets of medieval London must have been unbelievably sordid. When they were paved, which was by no means general, they were cobbled and the surface sloped inward from the sides to a runnel down the middle. There were no pavements for pedestrians; these were not considered necessary until the comparatively modern method of draining the roadway from the centre to gutters at the sides was introduced.

Householders were supposed to bring their slops out of the house and empty them into the runnel, but often the temptation to throw them out of an upper window was too great. Kitchen refuse was thrown out to rot in piles in the streets, blocking up the channels and sometimes causing foul-smelling floods which would seep over the door sill if the housewife had not taken the precaution of fitting a foot-high board in the doorway to prevent it. The butchers did their slaughtering in the streets, and the offal and blood added to the awful tide. You probably know that the Great Fire of 1666 broke out in Pudding Lane, running from Eastcheap down the hill towards the river; but the name apparently has nothing to do with the cooking of delectable puddings. The 16th-century chronicler Stow says it was so called because 'the butchers of Eastcheap have their scalding houses for hogs there, and their puddings and other filth of beast are voided down that way to the Thames dung boats'.

In those days of no refrigeration butchers and fishmongers could not hope to keep their wares fresh in warm weather, and this added to the noisome condition of London's streets.

This disgusting state of affairs was in no way due to neglect on the part of the city fathers. They did what they could, issuing innumerable ordinances against the fouling of the streets and taking action against offenders whenever possible, but almost to no avail. In this matter of cleanliness the medieval Londoner was his own worst enemy.

A scene from a medieval street: women shopping at a stall which sells belts and other leather articles.

There is a story of a man known as a rakyer who was employed by the ward of Cheapside to collect the dung and filth in the ward, but who found it easier to shove it over the boundary into the adjacent ward of Coleman Street! He was prosecuted, but this example could probably be multiplied a thousandfold. In 1421 another citizen was presented (that is, summoned) for 'making a great nuisance and discomfort to his neighbours by throwing out horrible filth on to the highway, the stench of which is so odious that none of his neighbours can remain in their shops'.

27

The City Corporation appointed scavengers to supervise street cleaning. Originally they had been Customs officials of the same standing as Chaucer was at one time, responsible for overlooking the unloading of imported goods at the wharves and quays. They were given the additional task of supervising the cleaning of the streets; then they were made responsible for the repair of the pavements; and later they undertook the supervision of fire precautions in new buildings. Carts were supplied to take the city's garbage to laystalls outside the walls, and boats to clear the rubbish from the riverside areas. By 1400 special days had been appointed on which household rubbish was to be put outside house doors for collection by the rakyers. But all these efforts were fruitless in the face of the citizens' lack of co-operation, and London remained an easy prey to the epidemics of plague and lesser visitations throughout the Middle Ages.

Although the City has been largely rebuilt several times and has received face-lifts in the way of road-widening here and there, many of the streets are still the same width as they were in medieval times. Walk along Cannon Street or King William Street and look down the side turnings. This, plus your imagination, will give you some idea of the roadways of medieval London.

Food

With 50,000 inhabitants, medieval London was a large and prosperous sales district for food producers, and its supplies came from a much wider area than the meadow and pasture immediately outside the walls. Also, a large tract north and east of the city was reserved as a royal forest ('forest' in this connection meant an uncultivated region used as a royal hunting ground and not necessarily a wooded area) and produced little in the way of food.

Meat

It is clear that meat was an important part of the diet, and cattle probably provided 60 per cent or more of it. The quality seems to have varied, from fat beef cattle reared for the market and driven long distances to be fattened and slaughtered in the London area to lean old plough oxen and worn-out cows from points nearer at hand. But all found a market, regardless of quality.

The supply of meat was seasonal because supplies of winter feed for cattle were very limited and many animals had to be slaughtered in the autumn. The medieval Londoner had no means of keeping meat fresh, so most of the surplus autumn meat was either smoked or

29

salted in casks of brine. Beef and mutton were usually salted, pork was often smoked for ham and bacon. Another problem was the provision of the large quantities of salt needed to preserve meat on such a scale, and some places on the coasts of Essex and Kent flourished on the extraction of salt from sea water. This led in turn to the slaughtering of cattle and their salting down for transport to London as ready-prepared meat.

Cooks at work preparing a banquet

Game and Poultry

Game such as deer, hares, and rabbits were a welcome source of fresh meat to relieve the winter monotony of salt meat, but it is doubtful whether anyone but royalty, nobility, and poachers tasted much venison—and the penalty for poaching deer from the royal forests was usually death. Domesticated birds were a more widely available source. Geese, ducks, and chickens were to be had all the year round. Pigeons were reared for eating, which accounts for the many handsome stone-built dovecotes one sees in the grounds of old manor houses and medieval monasteries.

Geese and ducks came to London 'on the hoof', so to speak, and to preserve the birds' feet on the march (what could one do with a lame duck—carry it?) they were first driven through wet tar or pitch spread on the ground and then through sand. This provided a 'sole' for their webbed feet and enabled them to complete the long trek from the country to London.

A 15th-century woodcut of a hunting party

Fish

Fish was an important item on the menu, apart from its obligatory use in Lent and on fast days. Apart from those caught in the Thames and numerous smaller streams in the district there were many artificial fishponds in palaces and monasteries, where species like carp and tench were bred, and where fish caught elsewhere could be kept alive until needed. Shellfish and crustaceans were popular; cockles, mussels, whelks, crabs, lobsters,

31

and shrimps were eaten, and of course oysters, which from the quantities of shell turned up during archaeological 'digs' seem to have been the most popular.

A great deal of dried and salted fish—cod, haddock, herring, and whiting particularly—was imported from Scandinavia, the Baltic, and the Netherlands.

Vegetables

It is clear that most of our modern vegetables were known in the Middle Ages, but there is very little evidence of their use. Root vegetables either were not often eaten or else they were considered so ordinary as not to merit any mention in the writings of the time. Apart from cabbage, beans, and peas, the only varieties which constantly crop up are onions, garlic, and leeks, and perhaps this gives us a clue. These strong-flavoured vegetables, together with many herbs some of which we would regard as weeds, must have been used to sharpen up the flavour of that dull old salt meat, or to disguise the fact that the fresh meat was a bit on the high side.

Peas and beans could be dried, and cabbage could be pickled, for use in the winter when nothing fresh was available.

Fruits

The medieval man-in-the-street ate much the same varieties of home grown fruit as we do, with the addition of some, like quince and mulberry, which are not common these days, but the foreign fruits which we accept as part of our normal diet—oranges, bananas, and so on—were not imported in the Middle Ages.

Dairy Produce

Dairy produce was an important element, but fresh milk was probably little used in London, as it would not keep or travel. Most of it would be made into cheese and butter on the farms. The yield of the medieval cow was small, and goats' and ewes' milk was used to supplement the butter and cheese making.

Bread

Although a lot of home baking obviously went on, it was by no means as universal as we might imagine, as can be seen from the many references to professional bakers and to the sizes, prices, and quality of loaves. This was probably due mainly to lack of suitable baking ovens in the smaller houses.

Drinks

Ale was the staple drink of everyone in the Middle Ages, but cider and perry were also available. Wine was imported in large quantities, much of it from the English territories in France, but it was not drunk in anything like the same quantities as ale, even in the wealthy households.

Cooking the Food

Most cooking was of course done on an open fire, and there were three methods: in a cauldron—which was very much more than just a big stewpot. It was in fact a medieval pressure-cooker in which several foods could be cooked in separate jars at the same time; baking in a closed oven—which we often, mistakenly, call roasting; and roasting proper on a turning spit before the fire.

A baking oven for bread and pies was found only in the bigger houses, and was quite separate from the open fire, from which it derived no heat though it might for convenience be alongside it. Built of brick and clay, the oven was pre-heated by making a fire inside it. When the right temperature had been reached, the fire and ash would be raked out and the bread, pies, or cakes put in to bake.

If the medieval housewife got tired of 'slaving over a hot stove' (and if her husband could afford it) she could always nip down the street and buy some of the many varieties of hot or cold cooked food which were on sale in the city.

The medieval housewife's 'pressure cooker': different types of food could be heated or cooked in separate containers inside a large metal cauldron.

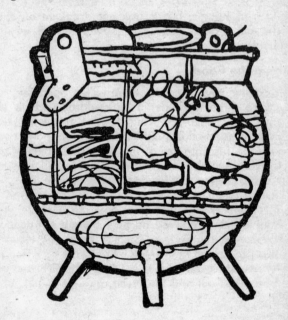

Water Supply

The provision of water for the citizens of London was a constant and growing problem as the population increased. The main sources in early medieval times were the numerous streams such as the Walbrook, the Fleet, and the Thames itself, and also many wells within the City. The situations of some of the wells is recalled by place- and street-names such as Well Court and Clerkenwell (the clerks' well)—but wells had a habit of drying up or becoming polluted. The river and its tributaries became more and more foul as the City grew, and many ponds which had earlier existed were drained and built over.

In the early 12th century the citizens had asked the king's permission to pipe water from Tyburn to the City, and by 1285 the Great Conduit in Cheapside was under construction. This was a big lead cistern with stone supports round it into which water was piped from Tyburn, probably through bored-out elm trunks, which were normally used for piping as they did not rot. The Conduit was fitted with brass taps at which the people could fill their buckets and casks. On festive occasions such as coronations, it is said the Conduit ran with wine—but basically what the Londoner wanted was water, if not for drinking, then for cooking and washing.

Other conduits were laid, but it was not until Elizabeth's reign that an enterprising Dutchman built the first watermill, or 'forcier', near London Bridge; this made use of the rush of water through the arches to provide pressure to pipe the water into the streets and houses. But by this time the river was so polluted that an Italian visitor described it as 'hard, turbid, and stinking'.

Even in the mid-19th century, when cast-iron mains were laid by the nine water companies then operating, the supply was turned on only for two or three hours three times a week.

One can appreciate that in the Middle Ages it must have often been impossible to wash oneself frequently, owing to lack of water, and it is no wonder that King John was regarded as rather peculiar because he had as many as eight baths in the short space of six months!

An example of medieval pottery: a small earthenware jug made in the shape of a man.

Language

From the Norman Conquest onward, three languages were used in England: Norman-French by the court and nobility, Latin by the Church and in official documents, and English by the common folk of Anglo-Saxon stock.

The first state document to be issued in English was the proclamation of Henry III's assent to the Provisions of Oxford (a constitutional document reforming the government of the country) in about 1269.

In 1362 Edward III's parliament enacted a statute terminating the use of French in the law courts, and in the same year the king made the first royal speech to Parliament in English.

By the end of Richard II's reign (1399) English had become the everyday language of the court, though one presumes that the king and his family, noblemen and bishops could all speak French as well. About twelve years earlier Geoffrey Chaucer had written his famous *Canterbury Tales,* one of the oldest surviving poems in English.

Traces of Norman-French still survive, however. For instance, the Queen's assent to parliamentary bills is announced in the House of Lords with the words 'La Reine le veult'—'The Queen wills it'.

The English accent in the Middle Ages, and indeed as late as Shakespeare's day, was not the Southern English speech we know today. It was much more akin to the Northcountryman's dialect. Muirhead's *Blue Guide to England* says of Langstrothdale, a remote valley at the head of Wharfedale in Yorkshire, that 'the dialect of this dale agrees more nearly than any other with Chaucerian English as used, for example, in the *Reeve's Tale*'. So if you would like to hear medieval English, go to Ilkley and drive northward up Wharfedale. Follow B.6160 from Threshfield to Buckden and turn left there onto an unclassified road into Langstrothdale!

The Government of the City

You all know, of course, that the City of London, commonly called simply 'The City', is the oldest part of the 700 square miles which make up Greater London; that it amounts to little more than 1 square mile itself; that its history goes back to the Roman days, when it was the major port and trading centre of the Province of Britain and the hub of the network of Roman roads which linked together all parts of the country; and that when William the Conqueror arrived in 1066 it was an important and flourishing city. Duke William, who was nobody's fool, realised that London needed special treatment, and so he granted to its citizens a charter—still in existence—confirming the rights they had enjoyed under Edward the Confessor.

Later, new privileges were granted to (or bought by) the Londoners, and in 1132 King Henry I, the Conqueror's son, issued a charter which recognised the status of London as a county and gave it the right of electing its own sheriff. This was indeed a privilege, since the sheriffs or 'shire reeves' were king's officers and appointed by him in all other counties of the realm.

Three figures which illustrate the development of armour in the Middle Ages. The man on the left wears the suit of chainmail and simple 'pot' helmet typical of the 13th century. By the 14th century (centre) metal plates had been added to protect the most vulnerable parts of the body, and by the 15th century this development had been completed (right) with the knight completely encased in armour which was jointed to allow him easy movement.

The Lord Mayor

The first mayor was Henry FitzAylwin, appointed in 1191 or 1192, and he remained in office until his death, twenty years later. Afterwards the mayors were elected annually, and in 1215 King John required each newly elected mayor to be presented to him or his justiciar (his chief adviser) for approval. The Lord Mayor for 1968-69 is the 641st holder of the office.

Within the City the Lord Mayor yields precedence to nobody but the Queen. The other members of the royal family, the archbishops, the prime minister, peers, and other dignitaries rank below him. This has been so for at least five hundred years. Outside the City he ranks as an earl and the state robes he wears at a coronation, for instance, are the scarlet and ermine of that rank.

Unlike all other cities and boroughs in England, London has no charter of incorporation, because it was already recognised as a thriving and stable community when such charters were invented. Magna Carta (1215) named the Mayor of London as one of those who were to see that the terms of the Charter were adhered to, and Edward I's parliament of 1295 (the first complete assembly of lords, clergy, and commons summoned by a king, though Simon de Montfort had called a similar meeting thirty years earlier) was mirrored in the government of the City by the two-chamber system of Court of Aldermen and Court of Common Council, the 'upper and lower houses' of the Corporation.

The Corporation

The governing body of the City consists of the Lord Mayor, twenty-five aldermen (an old title from the Saxon *Ealdorman*) and 159 Common Councilmen. Until the 17th century the Court of Aldermen alone ran the City, but from then on the Court of Common Council gradually took over most of the duties. However, the Common Council must still have the Lord Mayor (or his *locum tenens,* a senior alderman, and previous Lord Mayor) and two aldermen present to be effective.

Election of the Lord Mayor

The Lord Mayor is chosen by the Court of Aldermen

from names submitted by the liverymen of the City Companies, and serves for one year. The rather complicated selection procedure is described later.

Elecfion to Aldermen

The City is divided into twenty-five wards, varying in size from 6 acres (Bassishaw) to 149 acres (Farringdon Without; in this context 'Without' originally meant outside the City walls). Each ward elects one alderman, for life. Voters in the wardmotes must be residents, or owners or tenants of taxable property in the ward. Corporate tenants such as limited companies have no vote. There are about 15,000 voters in the city. All candidates for alderman must be freemen of the City (see below).

Election of Common Councilmen

Common Councilmen are elected by the wardmotes in the same way as aldermen, except that the number of Councilmen varies with the size of the ward and they are elected for one year only. They must be freemen of the City.

Election of Sheriffs

The City has two sheriffs (the second one was originally for Middlesex which was under the control of the Corporation), not appointed by the Sovereign but elected by the liverymen of the City Companies, like the Lord Mayor, for one year. The office of sheriff is much older than other municipal officers, going back at least to the 7th century.

Freedom of the City

Until the middle of the 19th century no one but a freeman was allowed to follow his trade or craft in the City. Freemen had certain privileges such as immunity from tolls at markets and fairs, and freedom from impressment into the navy or army. These days the privileges are limited to the widows and orphans of freemen and include admission to almshouses, free education, etc. However, it is still necessary for Common Councilmen and liverymen of the Companies to be freemen.

The Freedom can be acquired in three ways:

By **Servitude**	apprenticeship in a trade to a freeman.
By **Patrimony**	by reason of being the son or daughter of a freeman.
By **Redemption**	by purchase. Candidates for election by this method must be presented by a livery company or by the Court of Common Council.

The final decision rests with the Court of Aldermen, who also occasionally grant the Freedom to very distinguished people as the City's highest honour.

How to Become Lord Mayor of London

Here is a short guide for would-be Dick Whittingtons:

1. Apply for election as a freeman of one of the Livery Companies.
2. Acquire the Freedom of the City (see above).
3. Now you must move up in the hierarchy of your Company and acquire 'the livery'—a sort of superior membership. Acceptance is dependant on the decision of the Court of the Company and upon the number of liverymen allowed, which is a matter for the Court of Aldermen.
4. The next step is to be elected Common Councilman by the wardmote of the ward in which you are a resident or ratepayer.
5. Now you must be elected alderman of a ward—not necessarily your own in this case. You will be elected for life but if you find the going too hard you *can* resign.

6. At some stage in your municipal career you must be elected as one of the two City sheriffs, one of whom is an alderman and the other not. The liverymen of the Companies, 'in Common Hall assembled', elect the sheriffs.

7. The way is now clear for your election as Lord Mayor —again by the liverymen. The Recorder reads the names of the candidates, which the liverymen greet with cries of 'All!', 'Next Year!', or 'Later!' The two names receiving most support are passed to the Lord Mayor and Aldermen, who then ballot. The first time your name is put forward you may expect it to be answered by 'Next Year!' and the alderman who is senior to you will be chosen. But never mind. If all goes well, at the next annual election your name will elicit shouts of 'All!' and you will be Lord Mayor of London—subject of course to the approval of the Lord Chancellor, acting on behalf of the Crown.

City Officers

Ceremonial Officers

The officers of the Lord Mayor's household who attend
him on ceremonial occasions are these:

The Swordbearer

who carries one of the City's five state swords in front of
the Lord Mayor. He also summons aldermen and common councilmen to the various courts and meetings. He
wears a splendid fur cap on all occasions—even in the
presence of the sovereign and in church. He was first
mentioned in 1419.

The Common Cryer and Sergeant-at-Arms

whose office dates from the 14th century, carries the
Mace on ceremonial occasions. He reads Royal Proclama-
tions, such as the announcement of the death or accession
of a sovereign, from the steps of the Royal Exchange.
He wears a robe and wig similar to that of a barrister.

The City Marshal

who dates back to 1595, precedes the Lord Mayor on
state occasions—indoors on foot, and in carriage proces-
sions on horseback. He wears a scarlet tail coat and a
cocked hat with plume.

City Chamberlain

This ancient office, which can be traced back at least to the 13th century, corresponds to the City Treasurer in other English municipalities (though the Scottish burghs use the title of Chamberlain). He has other special duties such as custody of the City's 'private income', which derives from legacies, property, and other sources and is known as City's Cash. This is the fund which finances the Lord Mayor's Show, the Banquet, entertainment of foreign heads of state, and many other functions, at no cost to the ratepayers of the City.

The annual amount of rates levied by the Chamberlain on the City is about £22,000,000, of which about £15,000,000 goes to the Greater London Council and the Inner London Education Authority. The remaining £7,000,000 is for the City's own needs in the way of highways, police, and rebuilding.

The Chamberlain also admits Freemen of the City, enrols apprentices, and settles disputes between them and their masters, if required.

The holder of this office in 1968 is Mr. Charles Richard Whittington!

Town Clerk

The City has a Town Clerk like any other municipality (though his office goes back further than most—to 1274). Apart from his usual duties he is also Keeper of the Records of the City; these archives, covering nearly nine centuries of municipal activity, are the most complete and valuable series of such records in existence.

Comptroller and City Solicitor

Vice-Chamberlain and also legal adviser to the Lord Mayor and the Commissioner of Police for the City. He prosecutes at trials of offences committed in the City.

The Remembrancer

This official's duties are threefold: parliamentary, ceremonial, and legal. He is the channel of communication between the Corporation and the Government at Westminster, prepares private bills presented to Parliament by the City, and presents the City's petitions at the bar of the House of Commons. He has free access to M.P.s and to the lobbies of the House. The Remembrancer is responsible for the organisation of ceremonial occasions, such as Guildhall banquets and the Lord Mayor's Show. Another of his duties is to ensure that the City's ancient rights and privileges are not infringed by any outside body.

Other Officers

The City has the usual municipal officers, of course, but we have space here to mention only one who is in a rather special position—the Medical Officer of Health. Under the Public Health Act of 1872 the City is responsible for health matters in the Port of London, and the Medical Officer's jurisdiction runs from Teddington to the Tongue Light Vessel off Margate—a distance of over 90 miles. The control of communicable disease, inspection of food imports, and hygiene in ships and dock areas all come within his sphere. When we realise that London is the third largest port in the world and sees the arrival or sailing of about two hundred ships a day, we see what a gargantuan task he faces.

City Occasions Open to the Public

The Lord Mayor's Show
This is a combination of two former ceremonies, both going back over six hundred years. One purpose of the Procession is to identify the new Lord Mayor to the citizens; the other is for him to be presented at the Law

Courts to the judges of the Queen's Bench and to make his final declaration before taking office.

The Procession takes place on the second Saturday in November. It goes from the Mansion House to the Law Courts in the late morning, and returns by way of Victoria Embankment about 1.0-1.30 pm. There are military bands, lots of tableaux on floats depicting a theme chosen by the Lord Mayor, and he comes last of all in his great state coach, pulled by the splendid shire horses of Whitbread's brewery.

Election of the Lord Mayor, Michaelmas Day (29 September).

Election of Sheriffs, Midsummer Day (24 June).

These two functions take place in Guildhall, and there is limited accommodation for the public.

Declaration of Office by the Lord Mayor on the day before the Show, in Guildhall. Known as the 'Silent Change' because very little is said during the ceremony of handing over the City insignia to the new Lord Mayor.

Times and other details of these ceremonies can be obtained from the City Information Centre, on the south side of St. Paul's Cathedral.

The Livery Companies of London

These venerable institutions were once known as 'Gilds', from an Old English word meaning a yield or payment. In their earliest form they were friendly or mutual aid societies—'benefit and burial clubs'—or for various public services such as the collection of funds to maintain bridges or help lepers. Trinity House is a present-day survivor of this type; originally formed to collect alms for the provision of warning lights around the Thames estuary, the Brethren now control all navigational aids in English and Welsh coastal waters.

Each of these early guilds of social or religious character was established in its own quarter of the city and was usually connected with a particular parish church. Because the men engaged in a particular craft or 'mistery' tended to settle in the same street or area, each guild gradually became identified with the trade carried on by its members—witness this extract from the records of the Grocers' Company:

It was agreed that none should be of the fraternity if he were not of good condition and of their mistery, that is to say a pepperer of Soper Lane, or a canvasser of the Ropery, or a spicer of Cheap, or other man of their mistery wherever he might dwell.

In time the guilds acquired the right to control the entry of apprentices into their trades, to fix wages and prices, and to set standards of workmanship. At the end of this chapter is an extract from the Articles of the Cordwainers' (shoemakers') Company as submitted to the mayor and aldermen for approval in 1375.

As the influence of the companies in their own trades increased, so did their participation in the government of the City and eventually they acquired the right—which they still have—of electing the Lord Mayor and the Sheriffs of London. The companies were also authorised to wear a distinctive dress or livery—hence the name.

A reminder of medieval street signs: the modern one outside Cutlers' Hall.

The means by which they imposed standards of quality and honesty on their members were always appropriate and often pretty rough. A baker of short-weight loaves would find himself in the pillory with the offending merchandise strung round his neck, a butcher caught selling bad meat would have it burnt under his nose, bad wine was often poured over the vendor's head. A goldsmith who sent a piece of inferior craftsmanship to Goldsmiths' Hall would have it returned to him clipped in two. A member of the Stationers' Company who published a version of the Bible with an unfortunate error— he omitted the word 'not' from the commandment forbidding adultery—was fined £500 and the copies of the so-called 'Wicked Bible' were burnt outside Stationers' Hall.

The companies employed Wardens of Search who were empowered to enter the premises of their members and inspect their goods. It was insisted that liverymen should be 'masters' of their trade, that is self-employed, and both makers and sellers of their goods. Conformity to the terms of indenture of apprentices was enforced, and a master failing to fulfil his side of the bargain in housing, feeding, clothing, and teaching his apprentices might have the boys taken out of his charge by the company and indentured to a new master. The normal apprenticeship was for seven years, but in some cases it was longer; in the 1490s the Grocers' Company insisted on ten years.

As the years rolled by the livery companies became more and more influential in the government of the City, and more and more monopolistic in the control of their trades. Their members were exempt from payment of tolls such as lastage (for participation in fairs and markets), pontage (bridge maintenance), murage (repairs to the city walls), and pavage (road maintenance). Foreigners were excluded from membership. Even among their own members discrimination was sometimes practised, for instance by the introduction of an elaborate livery which was *de rigueur* at company meetings but which was too expensive for some members to buy.

Gradually the old principle that every liveryman should be his own master was abandoned, and an increasing number of journeymen appeared—fully trained in their craft but nevertheless hired workmen. The apprenticeship system, admirable in principle, had become oppressive, stifling initiative and imposing rigid conformity.

The livery companies were at the height of their power and influence in the 14th and 15th centuries, but by Tudor times their sun was setting. The 16th century saw a great diminution in their importance, partly because London was growing beyond its medieval walls and craftsmen were settling further out, where the City's writ did not run; partly because of the rise of capitalism and its effect on the self-employed 'master'; and partly because of the introduction of 'patrimony', whereby the son of a liveryman could join his father's company without having served an apprenticeship in the trade.

The disastrous fire of 1666 destroyed much company property, and also caused even greater numbers of liverymen to move out of the City. Later, the founding of 'journeymen's clubs' as a sort of poor man's livery company—perhaps the beginning of trade unionism?—further undermined the monopoly of the livery. During the 17th and 18th centuries their control dwindled more, and now only a few of them exercise any control at all over their ancient crafts.

The Goldsmiths' Company still acts on behalf of the

A contemporary woodcut of a carpenter and his tools

Crown as the London assay office, all articles made by goldsmiths and silversmiths having to be endorsed as of the quality claimed by being sent to Goldsmiths' Hall for 'hall-marking'. They also have the duty of carrying out an annual testing of coins produced by the Royal Mint, known as the Trial of the Pyx; representative coins of all types are tested, cupro-nickel as well as gold and silver. The Gunmakers operate a proof house in Whitechapel Road for the testing of gun barrels. The Fishmongers have a Fish Meter (the old Warden of Search) who can, and still does, control the quality of fish sold at Billingsgate Market; only a year or two ago a firm there was prosecuted by the Meter for selling undersized lobsters! The Apothecaries are an examining body which grants diplomas in medicine, surgery, and midwifery.

Many companies, however, are no longer active in their trade and are concerned only with educational and charitable matters. All the companies have a great reputation in this field; the joint income of all the companies is about £800,000 a year and most of this is spent, not in riotous living and huge, indigestible livery dinners but on maintaining schools (forty of them altogether) and charities (of which there are scores).

The companies have had their differences from time to time. The Skinners and the Merchant Taylors had an argument about precedence in the 15th century, each claiming to be sixth in seniority. King Richard III settled the matter by ordaining that the two companies should alternate each year between Numbers Six and Seven in the table of precedence (could this be the origin of 'being at sixes and sevens'?) and directed the Skinners to entertain the Merchant Taylors to dinner on the feast of Corpus Christi, and the Merchant Taylors to be hosts to the Skinners on the feast of St. John the Baptist. This fixture is still kept, of course.

Centuries ago the Armourers and the Braziers had a demarcation dispute about which company should make brass armour, and sensibly solved it by amalgamating.

The Vintners and Dyers also quarrelled. Each had a right to ownership of the swans on the Thames and each claimed three quarters of the total number of new birds. The Crown was asked to adjudicate and did so, awarding a quarter to the Dyers, a quarter to the Vintners—and taking the remaining 50 per cent to itself as an arbitration fee! Ownership of swans on the river is still in the same hands, and that is why the Queen's Swanmaster joins those of the two companies in the annual ceremony of swan-upping every July, when all cygnets found between London Bridge and Henley are marked as the property of one or other of the three owners—one 'nock' or nick on the beak for the Dyers' birds, two for the Vintners', and none for the Queen.

In the 14th century every member of the Wax Chandlers' company had to supply one pound of candles to St. Paul's cathedral; the company still keeps the church in candles for the altar.

The Skinners, alone among the companies, have a special way of conducting the annual election of their Master. All possible candidates assemble and pass round a tatty old cap which they try on. Then 'who so the cap fits, wears it' and becomes Master for the ensuing year. Strangely enough, the cap always fits the Senior Warden.

Although many medieval trades have died out the companies concerned with them have moved with the times. The Fanmakers, who used to make lovely fans of silk, ivory, and so on for elegant ladies, now have numbers of ventilation engineers among their number; and the Horners, once concerned with the making of plates, mugs, and windowpanes from horn, now include some plastics manufacturers.

Some of the companies' names are now archaic. Here are some translations:

Cordwainers Workers in Cordovan Leather—shoemakers.

Girdlers	Nothing to do with female foundations, but makers of belts with pouches, worn in the days when men's clothes had no pockets.
Loriners (or **Lorimers**)	Makers of the metal parts of horse-furniture, such as bits.
Fletchers	Arrow-makers.
Chapemakers	Makers of metal tips for sword scabbards, etc.
Lateners	Workers in brass.
Tapicers	Tapestry makers.
Hurers	Hatters.
Limners	Artists.
Upholders	Upholsterers.
Ferrours	Iron workers.
Stationers	Fixed-location booksellers, as opposed to itinerant sellers.
Grocers	Began as Pepperers, then turned to wholesale trade, hence Grossers or Grocers.

In 1422 there were one hundred and eleven companies active in London. Now there are eighty-four. The twelve senior companies are known as the 'Great Companies' and here they are in order of precedence:

1. Mercers
2. Grocers
3. Drapers
4. Fishmongers
5. Goldsmiths
6. Skinners   { Alternating
7. Merchant Taylors   { each year
8. Haberdashers
9. Salters
10. Ironmongers
11. Vintners
12. Clothworkers

Many of the livery companies have magnificent halls, but most of them are modern since the various disasters to the City—such as the Great Fire and the Blitz—have taken their toll. The only medieval remains are the crypt of the Mercers' Hall. Some halls are open to the public on certain days in the summer, but prior application is necessary. You can find out which halls are open, and when, from the City Information Centre, just across the road from St. Paul's Cathedral (south side). The livery halls, with their fabulous collections of plate and other treasures, are well worth a visit.

An 'acquamile' or water container made in the shape of a mounted knight of the 13th century—British Museum.

Extract from the Articles of the Cordwainers, as proposed in a petition to the Mayor and Aldermen in 1375.

'In the first place—that if anyone of the trade shall sell to any person shoes of bazen [sheepskin tanned in oak or larch bark] as being cordwain [Spanish shoe leather], or of calf-leather for ox leather, in deceit of the common people, and to the scandal of the trade, he shall pay to the Chamber of the Guildhall, the first time that he shall be convicted thereof, forty pence; the second time, half a mark; and the third time the same, and further, at the discretion of the mayor and aldermen.

Also, that no one of the trade shall keep house within the franchise [that is the City] if he be not free of the City and one knowing his trade, and that no one shall be admitted to the freedom without the presence of the wardens of the trade bearing witness to his standing, on the pain aforesaid.

Also—that no one of the trade shall entice or purloin the servant of another from the service of his master by paying him more than is ordained by the trade, on the pain aforesaid.

Also—that no one shall carry out of his house any wares connected with his trade for sale in market or elsewhere except only at a certain place situated between Sopereslane [Sopers = soapmakers]—the site of the present Queen Street, Cheapside—and the Conduit [water fountain, London's main water supply]; and that at a certain time of day. . . .

Also—that no one shall expose his wares openly for sale in market on Sundays at any place, but only within his own dwelling to serve the common people, on the pain aforesaid.'

The Jews

In the Middle Ages the Church condemned the lending of money at interest as sinful, so it was not possible for a Christian to be a usurer or money-lender. The Norman kings encouraged Jewish immigration so that they might operate as such—a very necessary social service, not least for kings, for most of them were perpetually short of ready money!

The Jewish communities, settling in such cities as London, Winchester, Lincoln, Norwich, and York, were under the protection of the king, though this did not always insure them against savage attack. There was always enmity between Christian and Jew, stemming in part from the time and spirit of the Crusades, and this often rose to boiling point and exploded into violence against the Jewish minority. It cannot be doubted also that an important motive on these occasions was the determination of the Jews' debtors to destroy all record of their indebtedness, which owing to the enormous rates of interest charged, often as much as 80 per cent to 100 per cent per annum, was crippling.

There were massacres of Jews in London at the time of Richard Lionheart's coronation, followed by others at

Lincoln, Norwich, and King's Lynn. At York, in 1190, anti-Jewish persecution led to their taking refuge in the royal castle, where they first destroyed their possessions, then set fire to the building and killed themselves and each other sooner than abandon their faith—a demand frequently made by their persecutors. Such survivors as asked for mercy were promised it by the mob, but as they emerged they were cut down to the number of just over one hundred.

Jews, though at most times tolerated by authority and allowed to operate as usurers, were liable to extortionate taxation, had no civic rights, were forbidden to carry arms even for their own defence, and could not own inheritable landed property.

The Jewish quarter in the City of London was in the area now indicated by the street named Old Jewry, running north from a point near the junction of Cheapside and Poultry.

Henry III, always zealous for the Church, founded a home for Jews converted to Christianity. Converts were required to give up their property in exchange for an allowance of 1½d a day for men, or eightpence a week for women, take a Christian name, and move into the so-called House of Converts, which stood in Chancery Lane on the site of the present Public Records Office. This charitable act, however, did not inhibit Henry from extracting large sums of money from the Jews in about 1250, nor from approving a statute in 1269 forbidding them to acquire debtors' lands.

The House of Converts was not a howling success and few converts came forward. Not surprising, really, since Henry's son Edward I had had all Jews in England arrested in 1278 for 'clipping the coin', and in 1290 they were banished from the kingdom, Edward having apparently decided that they were now squeezed dry! The House was closed by Edward III in 1377 and given to the Master of the Rolls, the judge charged with the custody of state records—which is why the Public Records Office stands there now.

The Jews were not readmitted to England until the 17th century.

After the expulsion of the Jews the business of money-lending in London passed into the hands of Italian and French merchants—the Lombards and the Caursines. Though Christians, it seems they had no inhibitions about the Pope's ban on usury—they were, after all, the main collectors in Europe of the papal revenues! Lombard Street, close to the Royal Exchange and Mansion House, recalls their place of business, and is still mainly inhabited by bankers. Recently the medieval custom of hanging out decorative signs has been revived in Lombard Street, and it is well worth a visit to see these attractive 'advertisements'.

A carved ivory draughts piece

Education in the Middle Ages

In Norman and early medieval times formal education was only for the favoured few—almost exclusively churchmen. There had been earlier attempts by enlightened people like Alfred the Great to bring the benefits of literacy to a wider section of the community—he encouraged scholars of European reputation to come to England, founded a court school for the education of the nobility, and even translated certain great works from Latin into Anglo-Saxon himself, thus establishing the first 'native' literature in England.

But Alfred was exceptional, and for centuries after his time the mysteries of reading and writing were left to the Church—the 'clerks in Holy Orders'. Indeed, the Norman and early Plantagenet kings and their noblemen may have regarded such accomplishments as rather sissy, and no fit pursuits for virile fighting men. Certainly William the Conqueror could not even sign his name; charters issued by him which still survive were 'signed' by him with a cross.

There seem to have been schools attached to monasteries from an early date, but the main if not the only purpose of these was to train boys as choristers and for the priesthood.

By the 14th century, however, it is clear that grammar schools existed for the education of boys who were not destined for the church. We have little direct knowledge of these establishments, but it is evident from many wills and other documents that there were numbers of them. The extreme shortage of books before the introduction of printing by Caxton in 1476 probably dictated the form of the school, and the picture brought to mind is that of a priest or deacon reading and talking to a small group of boys as they sit on hard benches, or cross-legged on the floor, the master teaching by word of mouth and the pupils learning their lessons by heart.

Most of these schools, it seems, were 'private' schools in the sense that the education of the boys was paid for by their parents.

Probably as an aftermath of the Black Death, many grammar schools in England had closed by about 1400; some estimate the number as high as seventy. The situation was thereafter restored by many public-spirited citizens and corporate bodies such as the Livery Companies, who founded new schools by donation or legacy.

For example, in 1442 John Carpenter, citizen of London and a friend of Sir Richard Whittington, bequeathed the rent from certain land and tenements for the maintenance and education of four boys who were to serve as choristers in the Guildhall chapel, being boarded in the 'college' of the chapel. This college was in fact the quarters of the priest who served the chapel; it was dissolved in 1547, soon after the Dissolution of the monasteries.

For another three hundred years, however, four 'Carpenter Children' continued to be maintained and educated under the terms of the bequest. Then, in the 19th century, Carpenter's property had increased so much in value that the City Corporation decided to put it towards the building of its own City of London School —now an important and respected boys' school and one of the many in England founded in the same way. There are still four Carpenter Scholars who receive free education and a maintenance allowance under John Carpenter's original bequest. The City of London School is now on Victoria Embankment, close to Blackfriars Bridge.

Many of the Livery Companies have founded schools, or taken over responsibility for the running of schools founded by their liverymen, and they also provide numbers of scholarships at schools and universities.

However much the educational system in England has changed since the Middle Ages, it seems that the beneficiaries (or victims) of it, the boys, have not. Here is an extract from the rules laid down for the conduct of the inmates of a school attached to Westminster Abbey in the 13th century:

Then, after they have made up the beds properly, let them leave their room together quietly, without clattering, and approach the church modestly and with washed hands, not running, or skipping, or even chattering, or having a row with any person or animal; not carrying bow or staff, or stone in the hand, or touching anything with which another could be harmed; but marching along simply and honestly and with ordered step . . . those who break these rules will feel the rod without delay.

Again, whoever at bedtime has torn to pieces the bed of his companions, or hidden the bedclothes, or thrown shoes or pillows from corner to corner, or roused anger, or thrown the school into disorder, shall be severely punished in the morning.

In 1385 the Bishop of London found it necessary to threaten with excommunication boys who:

. . . good for nothing in their insolence and idleness, instigated by evil minds and busying themselves rather in doing harm than good, throw and shoot stones, arrows, and different kinds of missiles at the rooks, pigeons, and

other birds nesting in the walls and porches of the church (St. Paul's Cathedral) and perching there. Also they play ball inside and outside the church and engage in other destructive games there, breaking and greatly damaging the glass windows and the stone images of the church, which, having been made with the greatest skill, are a pleasure to the eyes of all beholders, adorning the fabric and adding to its refinement. This they do not without great offence to God and our church and to the prejudice and injury of us as well as to the grave peril of their souls.

The Universities

For centuries there were only two universities in England, Oxford and Cambridge. They both originated in the 12th and 13th centuries (though the towns themselves are older) and both may have sprung from the schools attached to monastic establishments there. Perhaps their development was aided by the expulsion of English students from the University of Paris, then the centre of European learning.

The colleges, founded from the mid-13th century onward as self-governing corporations with their own royal charters, were almost entirely reserved for what we call nowadays graduate members (as All Souls, Oxford, still is), and the early students—all churchmen, of course, or destined for the church—found lodgings where they could. The greed of the townspeople and the high prices they charged for food and accommodation led gradually to the establishment of hostels, or 'halls', run by graduate teachers, where the young men could live communally and as cheaply as possible. It was not until the 16th century that the undergraduates were admitted to full membership of the colleges and the universities took on their present residential form.

Pilgrimage

The custom of making pilgrimages to holy places, usually the tombs of saints credited with healing properties, was very much a part of medieval life. There were many places of pilgrimage in England—the tomb of St. Edward the Confessor at Westminster, the shrine of Our Lady of Walsingham, the tombs of St. John of Beverley, St. Swithin of Winchester, and King Henry VI at Windsor are a few of them—but undoubtedly the most revered and popular objective for a pilgrimage was the shrine of St. Thomas Becket in Canterbury cathedral. After his death in 1170 a constant stream of pilgrims made their way there, not only from every corner of England but from the Continent too.

Travellers from the north of England would probably make their way via London and would join the Cockney pilgrims at the inns of Southwark, which specialised in the pilgrim trade, before starting their journey down the old drovers' road into Kent. Pilgrims from the west and south-west, and some continentals, would follow the route now known as the Pilgrims' Way. This track runs along the southern slopes of the North Downs from the vicinity of Winchester almost to Canterbury. In places it is still in use as a modern road—for instance, the un-

The tomb of Rahere: St. Bartholomew the Great, Smithfield

bove: Traitors' Gate at the Tower of London
eft: South side of the White Tower

Above: *One of the medieval cloisters in the Abbey*
Left: *Westminster Abbey, the nave and portrait of Richard II*

Above: The Jewel Tower, Westminster
Left: The Court of the King's Bench in the 15th Century

British Museum manuscript: soldiers looting a town
Photographs except where specified are by Michael Taylor

classified road from Otford (on A.225) to Wrotham (on A.20); elsewhere it is a bridlepath, and sometimes a mere track along the edge of a field. It is now accepted that the Pilgrims' Way antedates the pilgrims by many centuries and is in fact a prehistoric trackway possibly 3,000 years old.

But let us return to the Londoners' route. It was the custom to congregate at the inns in Southwark which, being outside the City gates, allowed of an early start before the gates were opened for the day. One of the most notable pilgrim inns was the *Tabard*, which stood on the corner of Borough High Street and Talbot Yard. Its site is marked by a plaque.

The pilgrims used to travel to Canterbury in groups, to afford each other mutual protection from footpads and thieves on the journey, and the diversity of type among the pilgrims is evident from Chaucer's characters in his *Canterbury Tales*.

The social and 'holiday' atmosphere of pilgrimage cannot be denied, but the pilgrims' spiritual needs were also taken care of, and numerous chapels existed along the routes to Canterbury where they could hear Mass during their journey. They took from two to four days to reach Canterbury, depending on their mode of transport, the distance being about 60 miles.

If the city gates of Canterbury were closed when they arrived they would stay the night at inns built for this very purpose outside the walls. The 16th-century 'House of Agnes' on the right, and probably the *Falstaff Inn* opposite, are survivors. From the West Gate of the city (the only one left of six) the pilgrims would follow the main street as far as Mercery Lane leading off left to the cathedral, and on the way they would pass St. Thomas' Hospital, a hostel for poor pilgrims. This has a fine 12th-century crypt, where you can see the hard stone benches on which they slept.

Mercery Lane, by all accounts, was something of a

tourist trap—or perhaps we should say pilgrim trap. Here were shops and stalls selling all manner of souvenirs, from phials of holy water from Becket's Well in the cathedral crypt to badges, medallions and statues of St. Thomas. Most pilgrims, except the very poorest, would buy something here to take home, and one imagines that a pitch in Mercery Lane was a much-sought-after trading site.

A badge made of pewter, worn by pilgrims to the shrine of St. Thomas à Becket

There are examples of pilgrim badges in the Guildhall, British, and London Museums. They were usually made of lead or poor quality pewter.

The pilgrims would also be expected to give alms inside the cathedral after they had prayed at the martyr's tomb, and over the years these contributions provided vast sums for the enrichment of churches lucky enough to house a pilgrim shrine. For instance, the tomb of the murdered Edward II in Gloucester Cathedral (he had been refused burial by the short-sighted monks of Bristol and Malmesbury) drew so many pilgrims that their alms financed most of the rebuilding of the Cathedral, the first and one of the finest major Perpendicular buildings in England.

Some pilgrimages took the devout overseas to Rome, to the Holy Land, to the shrine of St. James of Campostela in Spain, and these must have been very costly journeys. Other pilgrimages were performed by proxy, as it were, and there are numerous instances of legacies being left for this purpose—'... to my son ten shillings to perform my pilgrimage to Walsingham ...'

A contemporary drawing of the squire from Chaucer's The Canterbury Tales

In some cases a vow to undertake a pilgrimage, which later turned out to be impossible or inconvenient, would be expiated by substitution, so to speak. Edward the Confessor built his great abbey of Westminster as a condition of the Pope's absolving him from his vow to make a pilgrimage to Rome.

The custom of pilgrimage went on, in spite of the scorn of the Lollards and other reformers, until the 16th century. Then, in the upheaval of Henry VIII's split from Rome, the dissolution of the monasteries and the spread of the Reformation, many saints' shrines were dismantled and looted, either by the king's representatives or by enterprising private citizens.

There is literally nothing left at all of Thomas Becket's shrine at Canterbury, a great empty space behind the high altar being the only indication of where it once stood. But it must have been magnificent in its time, as this description shows:

Not withstanding its great size [it] is entirely covered over with plates of pure gold; but the gold is scarcely visible from the variety of precious stones with which it is studded, such as sapphires, diamonds, rubies, balasrubies, and emeralds; and on every side that the eye turns something more beautiful than the other appears. And these beauties of nature are enhanced by human skill, for the gold is carved and engraved in beautiful designs, both large and small, and agates, jaspers and carnelians set in relievo, some of the cameos being of such a size that I do not dare to mention it.

Geoffrey Chaucer

Canterbury pilgrims inevitably bring to mind that famous Londoner, Chaucer, so a short article about him has been included in this book.

Religious Houses

Throughout the Middle Ages London remained the same size, girdled by its walls, though the writ of the Lord Mayor ran in Southwark, a 'liberty' or suburb of the City which had grown up round the south end of London Bridge. A few noblemen's and bishops' palaces had been built on the north bank of the Thames between Lud Gate and Westminster, but apart from these there was little building outside the walls except for the religious houses.

There were many of these, and together with some marshy and uninhabitable areas such as Moorfields they formed a kind of green belt round the City. They nearly all disappeared centuries ago, being seized, dispossessed or otherwise disposed of by various monarchs, and they are remembered now only by the names which survive in the districts where they once stood.

A friary of Dominicans (Black Friars, from the colour of their habits) stood about where the office of *The Times* newspaper now is, and the surrounding district took its name, as also did the later bridge nearby.

When the site for the *News of the World* building was being excavated, the remains of a Carmelite (White Friars) house were discovered, and you will find evidence of this in names of streets and buildings between Fleet Street and the Thames.

A little further west was the English headquarters of that great monastic crusaders' order of Knights Templar —the Temple. The order was suppressed in the 14th century and its lands were expropriated and given to the other 'fighting order', the Knights of St. John of Jerusalem, which was still in favour in England. The development of the king's permanent courts of justice at Westminster led to a great demand for lawyers' accommodation in the vicinity, and the Knights of St. John leased the Temple to the barristers, who formed there the Societies of the Inner and Middle Temple. They are still in possession.

The Order of St. John had another property just outside the City, the Priory of St. John at Clerkenwell. This order too was suppressed in due course, and nothing now remains of the priory but the gatehouse in St. John's Lane, north of West Smithfield.

Across the road from the Central Criminal Court ('Old Bailey'), close by the site of Newgate, was another friary, that of the Franciscans or Grey Friars, later to be occupied by the famous school of Christ's Hospital—the 'Bluecoat' School.

Other monastic or religious buildings included the Abbey of Bermondsey, much in favour in the Middle Ages as a retreat for royal ladies retiring from public life, and several bishops' palaces such as Winchester House in Southwark and Ely House, the site of which is now called Ely Place, off Holborn Circus.

There were also the great priory and infirmary of St. Bartholomew at West Smithfield, while close by was the Charterhouse (a monastery of the Carthusian order whose mother church was at Chartres). Further, there were several monasteries, nunneries and friaries in the eastern part of the City—St. Helen's, off Bishopsgate, Crutched Friars, and Austin Friars—whose names still appear on the street maps.

Kings of the Middle Ages

King	Period of Reign	Corresponding Architectural Period
John	1199 to 1216 ⎤	Early English Gothic
Henry III	1216 to 1272 ⎦	
Edward I	1272 to 1307 ⎤	
Edward II	1307 to 1327 ⎬	Decorated Gothic
Edward III	1327 to 1377 ⎦	
Richard II	1377 to 1399 ⎤	
Henry IV	1399 to 1413	
Henry V	1413 to 1422	
Henry VI	1422 to 1461 and 1470 to 1471	Perpendicular Gothic (Continues into 16th century under Henry VII and Henry VIII.)
Edward IV	1461 to 1470 and 1471 to 1483	
Edward V	2 months	
Richard III	1483 to 1485 ⎦	

The Kings of the Middle Ages

John

'To no one will we sell, to none will we deny or defer, right or justice' (Magna Carta).
Son of Henry II, brother of Richard Lionheart. Ruled from 1199 to 1216.

Sixteen years of misrule, involving the loss of the English territories in France, a four-year quarrel with the Pope over the election of a new archbishop of Canterbury which resulted in John's excommunication, and finally his tussle with the barons and bishops. This culminated in the latter forcing John to approve Magna Carta in 1215; the Great Charter was intended to restrict the king's power over barons and church, but the inclusion of some general 'civil rights' provisions enabled it to be interpreted later as a charter of civil liberties applicable to all the king's subjects.

Magna Carta was granted at Runnymede Meadow (on A.308 between Windsor and Staines). It was reaffirmed and reissued several times by later kings. Four copies of the original 1215 version still exist: two in the British Museum, one in Salisbury cathedral, and one in Lincoln cathedral. The Museum also has the barons' original draft of the Charter and the Papal Bull of August, 1215, condemning it.

The Mayor of London was named in Magna Carta as one of those appointed to ensure that the provisions of the Charter were adhered to.

John died at Newark and is buried in Worcester Cathedral. His tomb bears an effigy of him, at the feet of which lies a beast nibbling the point of his sword; this is supposed to be an allusion to the curtailing of the royal power by Magna Carta.

A 13th Century nobleman and his wife wearing the costume of the period which was still relatively simple and unadorned.

Henry III

Son of John. Ruled from 1216 to 1272.

Succeeded as a minor, the country being ruled by William the Marshal, Earl of Pembroke, as regent. When Henry came of age and married Eleanor of Provence his court was filled with her friends and relations, who soon attained tremendous power and influence. Simon de Montfort led a rebellion against these foreigners—although he was Henry's brother-in-law—and was successful at first. After defeating Henry at the Battle of Lewes he was the virtual ruler of England. Then he too alienated the English barons by his arrogance and ambition, and they, led by Henry's eldest son Prince Edward, defeated de Montfort at Evesham (1265) and reinstated King Henry—but insisted that he reaffirm and reissue Magna Carta.

Henry was no great success as a ruler. His greatest achievements were in building. Most of Westminster Abbey, and large parts of the Tower of London and Windsor, are his work.

He is buried in Westminster Abbey.

(See separate articles on the Abbey and the Tower.)

Edward I

Son of Henry III. Ruled from 1272 to 1307.

Edward's main aim throughout his reign was to secure and consolidate the kingdom and to establish a basis of sound law. He spent seven years subduing Wales and annexing it to England, and it was during this time that he built the great 'Edwardian' castles of Caernarvon, Conway, Rhuddlan, Harlech, Flint, and Beaumaris (see the separate article on medieval castles).

He also tried to subordinate Scotland, with the same object of securing England's frontiers, and had some success at first. In 1296 he defeated the Scots and reduced their country to the status of a dependency. Then, to

By the 14th Century the clothing of the rich was becoming
more decorated and ostentatious. Both men and women wore
bright colours, jewellery and ornaments.

show that he was their overlord, he took the ancient coronation stone of Scotland, the Stone of Scone, to Westminster and had the Coronation Chair made to hold it.

For a while Sir William Wallace led the Scottish opposition to English rule, but was eventually betrayed and captured. He was executed at West Smithfield, where you can see a tablet to his memory on the wall of St. Bartholomew's Hospital.

Edward I is also buried at Westminster. On the north side of his tomb you can still faintly see one of his nicknames, *Scotorum Malleus*—'Hammer of the Scots'. Sometimes he was called 'Longshanks'—he was over 6 feet tall.

A strong, just, and wise king.

Edward II

Son of Edward I, and the first to bear the title Prince of Wales. Ruled from 1307 to 1327; the first king to be crowned in the Coronation Chair.

This Edward was very prone to choose unsuitable people as favourites—often foreigners such as Piers Gaveston—and this antagonised the English barons.

The Scots rose again under Robert Bruce and Edward was heavily defeated at Bannockburn in 1314. Scotland regained her independence, which she was not to lose again until the union of the crowns in 1603.

Edward's queen, Isabella, and her lover Roger Mortimer schemed against the king, and in 1327 Parliament forced the king to abdicate in favour of his eldest son. Edward was imprisoned in Berkeley Castle (midway between Bristol and Gloucester) and was murdered there. He is buried in Gloucester cathedral.

Edward III

Son of Edward II. Ruled from 1327 to 1377.

Succeeded at fifteen years old. For four years his

During the 15th Century fashions became much more elaborate. Men's clothes were intricately trimmed and padded while
women wore tall headdresses and elaborate robes with wide
flowing skirts.

mother and Roger Mortimer ruled, but in 1330 Edward seized them both in Nottingham Castle, had Mortimer hanged, drawn, and quartered at Tyburn (bottom of Edgware Road, near the Marble Arch), and kept his mother locked up for the remainder of her life. There were two wars with Scotland during Edward's long reign, but the main event was his claim to the throne of France which initiated the Hundred Years War, in 1337.

The first major battle was at Crécy in 1346, when the Prince of Wales, afterwards known as the Black Prince, won his spurs at the age of sixteen. Soon afterwards Edward besieged and took Calais. This was the occasion on which he required the leading burghers of the town to appear before him with halters round their necks, intending to hang them; his queen Philippa is said to have pleaded successfully for their lives. There is a copy of Rodin's famous statue, *The Burghers of Calais,* in Victoria Tower Gardens, between the Houses of Parliament and Lambeth Bridge. (See separate article on a walk round Westminster.)

Edward III died in 1377, a few weeks after his eldest son, the Black Prince, and was succeeded by the latter's son Richard. Edward and his queen Philippa are buried in Westminster Abbey.

Richard II

Grandson of Edward III. Succeeded at the age of ten and had uncle-trouble for some years—the Black Prince's four brothers, Dukes of Clarence, Lancaster, York, and Gloucester, were forever telling him how to rule England.

In 1381 came the Peasants' Rebellion under the leadership of Wat Tyler. Later Richard, like others before him, fell under the influence of unpopular favourites, and in 1386 he was forced to yield the government of the country to a Council. But when he reached the age of twenty-two

Richard sacked the council and assumed sole authority. He became more and more authoritarian and oppressive, and in 1399 there was a rebellion led by Henry, Duke of Hereford (John of Gaunt's son). Richard was deposed in Henry's favour and imprisoned in Pontefract Castle, where he was either starved to death or murdered.

Later his body was brought to Westminster, where he shares a tomb with his first wife, Anne of Bohemia.

Henry IV

Son of John of Gaunt, Duke of Lancaster, and cousin to Richard II. Ruled from 1399 to 1413, the first Lancastrian king.

A troublous reign punctuated by war with the Scots and rebellions led by disaffected barons, notably the Percies, Dukes of Northumberland. As a usurper Henry doubtless realised the weakness of his position, and felt bound to rely on Parliament and the Church for support. In this reign the reforming religious sect known as Lollards were persecuted, the crime of heresy was first defined in English law, and the first Lollard was burnt at the stake.

King Henry is buried in Canterbury Cathedral, on the opposite side of the site of Becket's shrine from the Black Prince.

Henry V

Son of Henry IV. Ruled from 1413 to 1422.

More rebellions, this time led by the Earl of March, who had a better claim to the crown by descent than the Lancastrians. The Hundred Years War was resumed, the great victory of Agincourt was won (1415) by the English bowmen, and in 1420 it was agreed that Henry should succeed Charles of France on the latter's death. Henry married Charles' daughter, Catherine of Valois, but died in 1422, before the French king did. He is buried in Westminster Abbey. (See the separate article on the Abbey.)

Henry VI

Son of Henry V. Ruled from 1422 to 1461. A pious man, a great patron of learning and religion, but weak.

Henry VI came to the throne at one year old, and England was once again ruled by a council, with the king's uncle, Humphrey Duke of Gloucester, as Protector. Charles of France repudiated his treaty with Henry V, and the Hundred Years War was resumed. The English armies in France were soundly defeated by Joan of Arc, and over the next twenty years Henry lost all his French possessions except Calais. In 1453 he also lost his reason.

The rest of Henry VI's story is that of the Wars of the Roses.

Henry founded Eton College and King's College, Cambridge.

He is buried in St. George's Chapel, Windsor Castle. A move was set on foot to get him canonised as a saint, but the price demanded by the Pope was too high, and it came to nothing. You can still see an alms box beside Henry's tomb in which the numerous pilgrims to his tomb used to place their contributions.

Edward IV

Son of Richard, Duke of York, who touched off the Wars of the Roses. Ruled from 1461 to 1470 and again from 1471 to 1483. The first Yorkist king.

The first part of his life was occupied with the Wars of the Roses. From 1471 he ruled fairly well, but in his latter years he became gross and pleasure-loving and fell much under the influence of his mistress, Jane Shore.

He is buried in St. George's, Windsor, across the choir from his rival Henry VI.

Edward V

Son of Edward IV. Succeeded at thirteen years old and ruled in name only for two months. The elder of the two 'Princes in the Tower'.

After his father's death the young Edward, with his brother Richard, was held in the Tower of London, 'for his own safety,' by his uncle Richard, Duke of Gloucester. The boys were seen from time to time on the ramparts close to the Bloody Tower, where they were lodged, but after about two months they disappeared. It is still not established by whom they were disposed of, but the circumstantial evidence points most strongly to the Duke of Gloucester.

The floor of the upper room in the Bloody Tower where they were held has disappeared, so there is not much to see of their prison.

In the 1670s, during the demolition of a stairway on the south side of the White Tower, the bones of two children were found. Medical opinion of the time was that they were those of two boys of the right ages for the princes, and they were re-interred in a marble urn which you can see in the Queen Elizabeth Chapel, Westminster Abbey.

Richard III

Brother of Edward IV and uncle of Edward V. Ruled from 1483 to 1485.

After his brother's death, the Duke of Gloucester stated that Edward's marriage to Elizabeth Woodville had not been legal, since the king had been previously betrothed to a Lady Eleanor Talbot. In those days betrothal was as binding as marriage, and if this were so Edward's subsequent marriage would be invalid and the children of it illegitimate. On these grounds Parliament offered the crown to Richard of Gloucester who, after modestly declining for a while, accepted it.

In 1485 Richard III, as he was known, was defeated and killed at the Battle of Bosworth, near Leicester, by Henry Tudor, Earl of Richmond, who claimed the crown by reason of a distant descent from John of Gaunt.

Richard was buried at Greyfriars, near Leicester, but no trace of his grave remains.

Here we come to the end of the medieval period, Richard's successor Henry VII being the first of the Tudor dynasty.

Some Medieval Londoners

Geoffrey Chaucer

Geoffrey Chaucer was born in about 1340, the son of a London vintner. When he was sixteen or seventeen he entered the service of the Duchess of Clarence, a daughter-in-law of Edward III, and from then on he was on the fringes of the royal circle. Accompanying the Duke of Clarence on an expedition to France in 1359, he had the misfortune to be taken prisoner, but was ransomed the next year by King Edward. Sometime around 1365–70 Chaucer married Philippa, who was in the service of John of Gaunt's wife, the Duchess of Lancaster. Philippa's sister Catherine became John of Gaunt's mistress and later his third wife.

In 1367 he received a 'pension', more correctly an annuity, of 20 marks (£13. 6. 8.) from the king. From 1369 to 1370 he was abroad on the king's service, and in 1372–73 he went to Genoa and Florence on a royal errand. From 1372 onwards he was styled 'armiger' (esquire, entitled to have a coat of arms), and in 1374 he was given another pension of 20 marks by the king, and was appointed Comptroller of Customs in London. The same year John of Gaunt gave him a pension of £10 a year. From this time until 1386 he lived in chambers over Aldgate (one of the City gates) except when he was abroad on royal service. In the latter year he became Knight of the Shire, a sort of Member of Parliament, for Kent.

In 1388 he sold his two pensions from the king for ready cash. Perhaps he had been leading the high life, for he was now a widower. In the same year he went on pilgrimage to Canterbury.

In 1389 he became Clerk of the King's Works, and was in charge of the fabric of the Tower of London, the Palace of Westminster and eight other royal residences, five hunting lodges, the mews (where the king's falcons and hawks were kept) at Charing Cross, and all grounds attached to them. One distinguished man on his payroll was Henry Yevele, the master mason who restored Westminster Hall for Richard II, and who may have designed the new nave for Westminster Abbey; he also built the tombs of Richard II and probably Edward III.

In 1391 Chaucer was appointed royal forester for Somerset. In 1397 he received a new pension of £20 from Richard II, and two years later yet another one from Richard's rival and displacer, Henry IV, of 40 marks (£26. 13. 4.). He then leased a house in Westminster, but died the following year and was buried in the Abbey—probably because he had been Clerk of the King's Works, and not because he was a poet. You can see his tomb in the south transept, now known as Poets' Corner; the monument over his tomb was put up in 1555.

Geoffrey may have begun *The Canterbury Tales,* one of the oldest surviving poems in English, in about 1387, *before* he went on pilgrimage. The Tales purported to be those told by his fellow-pilgrims to while away the journey to Canterbury, but many of their themes were current in Europe at the time, and it seems probable that Chaucer had picked them up on his travels abroad on the king's service. *The Canterbury Tales* were first printed by Caxton in 1475.

William Caxton

The first English printer. Born in Kent in about 1422, he was apprenticed at the age of sixteen to a London mercer —a dealer in silks, satins, and other fine fabrics. After his master's death in 1441 he went to Bruges. Five years later he was in business on his own account there, and visited London again in 1453. From 1462 to 1470 he acted as governor of the English merchants in the Low Countries and negotiated commercial treaties with the Dukes of Burgundy during that time. While he was in Bruges he started to translate a French romance, *Le Recueil des Histoires de Troye,* and finished it in Cologne in 1471. Sometime in the next four years he learned printing, and may have owned a press in Bruges, for he printed two translations from the French in 1474–75.

A woodcut of the knight from an early edition of The Canterbury Tales

Caxton came to England in 1476 and enjoyed the patronage of Edward IV, Richard III, and Henry VII. He set up a press at Westminster, from which he issued over eighty books between 1477 and 1491, many of them translations by himself from the French. In 1485 he printed Sir Thomas Malory's collection of French stories about King Arthur—*Le Mort d'Arthur*.

In the British Museum manuscript room there is a copy of Caxton's first book, the *Recuyell of the Histories of Troy,* a first edition of *The Canterbury Tales,* and one of *Aesop's Fables*. He died in 1491.

Wynkyn De Worde

Another printer, this time a Londoner by adoption, as he was born at Worth in Alsace. He came to London and was apprenticed to Caxton at the press in Westminster. After Caxton's death he carried on the business, and in 1500 he moved the press to Fleet Street—perhaps the forerunner of all those generations of printers who have worked there since. In 1509 he opened a shop in St. Paul's Churchyard, where he sold the products of his press, and here he established another London precedent; until the bombing of the Second World War the precincts of the Cathedral, and especially Paternoster Row, were the home of numerous booksellers.

There is an interesting pub in New Fetter Lane called the *Printer's Devil,* where you can see a visual history of 'The Print' through the ages.

Sir Richard Whittington

Dick Whittington came to London, probably from Gloucestershire, and was apprenticed to a mercer. Having served his time he became a mercer himself, was active in the affairs of his livery company and the City, being elected to the Common Council in 1385 and again in 1387. In 1393 he became alderman for Broad Street ward, sheriff in 1394, and mayor in 1397, 1406, and 1419.

Whittington must have made his pile, for he is on record as having lent money to three kings—Richard II, Henry IV, and Henry V. One wonders whether he ever got it back! He was also a generous benefactor to the City, helped to finance the building of Leadenhall and the Guildhall Library, and left legacies for the rebuilding of Newgate Gaol and the foundation of an almshouse, which is still supported by his company, the Mercers.

One of his lesser known benefactions was the building in Vintry Ward, in 1419, of what must surely have been the biggest public lavatory ever heard of, with sixty places for men and sixty for women. Every ward in the City had its public latrine, but this must have excelled them all. Modern office regulations specify the provision of one lavatory for every fifteen employees, and by this yardstick Whittington took care of the needs of 1,800 citizens! This monumental edifice apparently survived until the great fire of 1666.

The legend about Dick Whittington's cat, that clever animal which helped him so much in his career, did not become connected with his name until the 17th century, and was treated with scepticism even then. Animal stories of this kind were common throughout Europe in the Middle Ages.

Sir Richard was buried in the church of St. Michael Paternoster Royal, at the foot of College Hill off Cannon Street. The name College Hill recalls the foundation of a college of priests attached to the church and founded by Whittington, which lasted until the Dissolution. The church was rebuilt after the 1666 fire, and is now being restored again after severe bomb damage.

An effigy of the Black Prince in Canterbury Cathedral

Eleanor Crosses

Eleanor of Castile was the daughter of King Ferdinand III of that country, and married Edward I of England before he succeeded to the throne. They were a devoted couple and Eleanor, refusing to be parted from her husband, accompanied him on all his travels, with the result that their children were born in the most unlikely places. One child was born at Acre, in Palestine, during the seventh Crusade; and the future King Edward II was born at Caernarvon Castle in Wales during a campaign against the Welsh.

It is said that during the Crusade Edward was wounded with a poisoned dagger by an envoy of the Emir of Jaffa, and that Eleanor saved his life by sucking the poison from the wound.

An effigy of Eleanor of Castile, wife of Edward I, in Westminster Abbey

In 1290 they were en route for Scotland when Eleanor died, at Harby in Nottinghamshire. The sorrowing Edward brought her body back to London by easy stages for burial at Westminster, and at each place where the body rested on its journey he later erected a memorial in the form of a Gothic pinnacle cross. There were originally twelve of them, but only three now survive—at Northampton, Geddington, and Waltham. The last halt was made in the little village of Charing between the City of London and Westminster, and a cross stood there—about where King Charles I's statue now is at the northern end of Whitehall—until it was removed by order of Cromwell's parliament in 1647. There is a modern replica (1863) in the forecourt of Charing Cross station. These memorials are now known as Eleanor Crosses.

Queen Eleanor is buried in the Confessor's Chapel in Westminster Abbey. It bears a somewhat idealised effigy of her, the work of the English goldsmith William Torel, who cast it in 1291. On the outer side of the tomb is a lovely iron grille, also of medieval English workmanship.

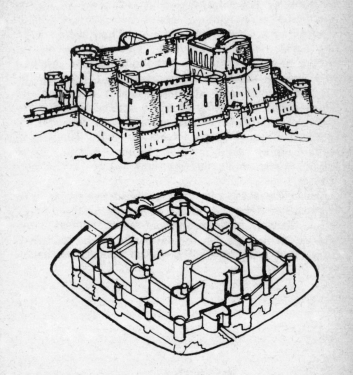

Two sketches which show the structural changes and development of castles during the Middle Ages. In both cases the earlier central keep has disappeared and been replaced by large and powerful gatehouses. The inner and outer curtain walls are interspersed with and protected by sturdy turrets.

Medieval Castles

The protection of buildings has been practised since man first began to build himself permanent homes. The Anglo-Saxon hall was fenced with a hedge or a wooden stockade, and wherever there was water available there would be a defensive ditch or moat.

Any prudent man planning to build a manor house in the Middle Ages would apply to the king for the necessary 'licence to crenellate', that is, to fortify his home. The amount of fortification, however, was usually small, probably consisting of no more than a surrounding wall with perhaps a gatehouse and a moat. The buildings within would remain largely domestic.

The castle proper was a different matter, defence being the first consideration and domestic comfort and convenience coming second. Many such castles were royal property and national in purpose, being designed and sited to defend the frontiers of the kingdom from outside attack. Durham and Ludlow castles, for instance, were there to repel attack over the borders from Scotland and Wales; Dover and Lewes castles covered possible invasion points and the routes leading inland from them; the Tower of London and Rochester castle had, among other functions, that of controlling important river crossings.

The earliest type of castle usually consisted of an artificial earth mound or 'motte' with a wooden building on it, surrounded by a ditch. The latter would be spanned by a movable wooden bridge. A larger area known as the bailey or ward, with an earth bank, palisade and ditch, enclosed the motte and was intended for the protection of the farm animals and the serfs and their families from the village nearby.

Later the wooden fort on the motte gave way to a hollow stone structure known as a shell keep (Arundel and Berkeley are examples of this), but sometimes it would be decided that the motte would not support the size and weight of a stone keep and another site would be chosen, and perhaps a bigger and more solid motte built. Perhaps the most impressive motte in England is at Thetford in Norfolk. It is 80 to 100 feet high and a 1,000 feet in circumference.

The earliest type of square stone keep belongs to the 11th and 12th centuries. Our two largest and perhaps finest specimens date from before 1100—the White Tower in the Tower of London, and Colchester Castle. Other square keeps within easy distance of London are at Rochester (Kent) and Hedingham (Essex).

With improved methods of siege, however, it was realised that the square keep, with its corner angles which could easily be undermined by tunnelling or by battering-ram, was too vulnerable, and so keeps were then built with multi-angular walls presenting much blunter and stronger corners.

Throughout the 12th century the curtain walls enclosing the bailey or ward became thicker and higher, with more and stronger towers along their length, enfilading the ground close to the face of the wall. By the next century the way was clear for the evolution of a quite new type of castle in which the keep entirely disappeared and was replaced by a big gatehouse containing the lord's living quarters and providing the strong point of the fortress, as the keep originally had done. These sturdy gatehouses were often extended outwards for greater strength, developing in effect into double gatehouses, which were known as barbicans. Bodiam castle in Sussex is a good example of a keep-less castle within easy reach of London. Warwick is another specimen of a later (14th-century) keep-less castle with barbican and flanking towers. The finest ones, however, are further afield—the so-called 'Edwardian' castles in North Wales, such as Conway, Caernarvon, or Harlech. These get their name from the fact that they were built by Edward I (1272 to 1307) during his Welsh campaigns.

Sometimes the curtain walls were duplicated, producing what is known as a concentric castle. Beaumaris in Anglesey is a fine example, albeit on the small side; the Tower of London is another, though this retains its older square keep in the centre.

You should remember, though, that all these impregnable-looking castles were built for defence against *men*, armed only with personal weapons such as sword, spear, axe, and bow, with perhaps a primitive form of artillery in the form of stone-throwing engines akin to the Roman *ballista*. The event which spelt their ultimate doom was the introduction of cannon. There was little chance of even the strongest medieval castle withstanding a prolonged bombardment by cannonfire, or undermining with gunpowder. So the era of the mighty fortress began to draw to its close in the 15th century, and warfare was soon to revert from an affair of siege and defence to the earlier form of mobile warfare.

The diminution in the military importance of castles was hastened in the Tudor days by the extension of the royal power and the consequent disappearance of the powerful feudal baron. From the 16th century onward many castles, though still inhabited, were adapted and made more comfortable to live in, at a sacrifice of their defensive strength. The final blow to most of them came after the Civil War of the 1640s when all castles which had been held for the defeated King Charles were 'slighted' by Cromwell—that is, reduced to ruin so that they could never again be refortified and used to defy the power of parliament.

Castles to See

Opening times and other information are shown in Appendix A

Tower of London. A concentric castle, but retaining its early Norman keep—the White Tower. The inner curtain walls with thirteen towers and the lower outer walls were built between 1189 and 1306. See *Walk Round the Tower of London* for details.

Colchester (Essex). Little remains of the medieval castle here except the Norman keep, but this is a splendid specimen. Built partly of Roman materials (you can easily recognise the flat Roman tile bricks in the walls), it is much bigger in ground area than the White Tower in London. It has been roofed in and contains a fine museum of very important Roman remains.

Rochester (Kent). The keep here is one of the finest in England, being still 120 feet high. It was built about 1130 by an Archbishop of Canterbury and stands inside an earlier wall by Bishop Gundulf, who also built the White Tower in London.

Hedingham (Essex). A huge Norman keep built about 1100 and still lived in. Privately owned.

Warwick (Warks.). A splendid specimen of a later keep-less castle (14th century) with massive towers on the curtain walls and a barbican. The living quarters inside were converted in the 17th century to a stately mansion with all manner of art treasures.

Bodiam (Sussex). Fine example of a smaller keep-less castle. Built about 1386 to cover a possible invasion landing-place—the river Rother was navigable as far up as Bodiam in those days—it sits in the middle of a wide moat full of water-lilies. The sturdy gatehouse takes the place of a keep. Although Bodiam is in ruin it is possible to climb the turrets and walls by several spiral stairways, and the place is a paradise for children.

Windsor (Berks.). The first fortress built on Windsor Hill was put up by William the Conqueror about 1070. It consisted of an artificial earth motte with a wooden fort on top. About a century later this wooden fort was replaced by a round stone structure. From these small beginnings grew the great castle of today. The Round Tower on the Conqueror's motte was raised and strengthened at various dates. The curtain walls of the Lower Ward, west of the Round Tower and sloping down to the town, were mainly built by Henry III in the 13th century. The Upper Ward, eastward of the Round Tower, contains the state apartments and the Queen's private apartments. The castle has been much altered many times in its long history, yet the essential parts of a medieval fortress—motte, keep, and bailey or ward—are still easily recognisable.

You may wonder why so obviously 'royal' a castle was not slighted after the Civil War. The reason is that, early on in the war, the castle was occupied without a struggle by the parliamentary forces and remained in their possession until their final victory over the Royalists. So Windsor Castle fortunately survived.

Thetford (Norfolk). Castle Hill at the east end of the town is the finest example of a Norman motte in England, 80 to 100 feet high and 1,000 feet round.

Arundel (Sussex). Very much restored and rebuilt, Arundel has an example of a shell keep.

Hever Castle (Kent). This is an example of a fortified manor house rather than a castle. Possibly the earliest and best specimen of this type is

Stokesay Castle in Shropshire; it has two towers of 1115 and 1284, a great hall, also 1284, between them, a gatehouse and a moat. If you are motoring between Hereford and Shrewsbury on A.49 you will find it about 3 miles south of Craven Arms.

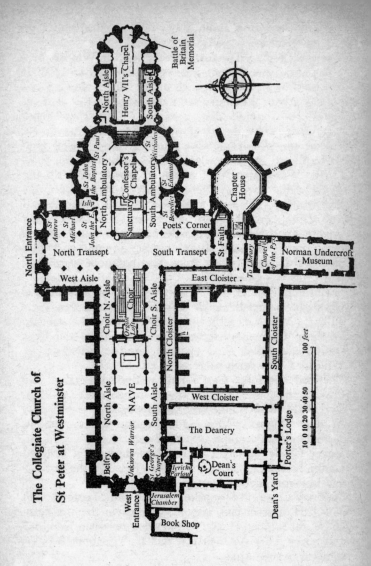

The Collegiate Church of
St Peter at Westminster

Battle of Britain Memorial

North Aisle

Henry VII's Chapel

South Aisle

St Paul

St John the Baptist

St Andrew

St Michael

St John the Ev.

Islip

North Ambulatory

St Nicholas

Confessor's Chapel

Sanctuary

St Edmund

South Ambulatory

St Benedict

Chapter House

North Entrance

North Transept

Poets' Corner

South Transept

St Faith

To Library

Chapel of the Pyx

Norman Undercroft Museum

West Aisle

East Cloister

Choir N. Aisle

Choir

Organ Loft

Choir S. Aisle

North Cloister

South Cloister

North Aisle

NAVE

South Aisle

West Cloister

Belfry

Unknown Warrior

St George's Chapel

The Deanery

Jericho Parlour

Dean's Court

Porter's Lodge

West Entrance

Jerusalem Chamber

Dean's Yard

Book Shop

100 feet

10 0 10 20 30 40 50

A Walk round Westminster Abbey

Legend has it that Sebert, King of the East Saxons, built a church in the desolate area then known as 'Thorneye', and that St. Peter himself miraculously appeared and consecrated it. But the first church here about which we are certain was built by King Edward the Confessor and consecrated on 28 December 1065.

Edward died in the early days of January 1066 and was buried in the church. About one hundred years later he was canonised as St. Edward, King and Confessor. The word 'Confessor' indicates a saint who was venerated for his piety but who was not martyred for his faith, as most saints were. After about another century, King Henry III decided to pull down the Confessor's Norman church and build a more splendid one as a fitting shrine for St. Edward, who was his own and England's patron saint. By 1269 the eastern end and the transepts were finished, and the nave was complete as far as the fifth bay (near the present organ). The western end was still the Confessor's Norman construction. It was not rebuilt in the Gothic style until many years later, and you can see the division between the old and the later work quite clearly; in the first five bays of Henry III's time, there is a decorative pattern known as diaper work in the spandrels (the roughly triangular spaces each side of the head of the arch), while the spandrels of the later western arches are plain.

On 13 October 1269 the new church was consecrated and the body of St. Edward was transferred from its old tomb to the splendid shrine behind the high altar, where it still is.

Starting the Walk

Here is a route round the Abbey, with particular emphasis on its medieval features. Start at the West Door—the Victoria Street end. Pause as you enter, and just *look*. The church has recently been cleaned inside and you can now see it as it should be seen—the pillars of grey Purbeck 'marble' and above them the soaring Gothic vaulting with its ribs and bosses picked out in gold—the highest medieval nave in England, just over 100 feet. The glorious chandeliers are modern, a gift from the Guinness family in 1965, and are of Waterford crystal. Although they are so up-to-the-minute in design they blend beautifully with the medieval building around them, and in fact they have an inverted Gothic shape of their own.

At a lower level the church is unfortunately cluttered with so many 17th and 18th century monuments that the unity of the Gothic building is obscured. For better or worse, these memorials are with us and we must put up with them; but when you tire of them, just lift up your eyes to the lovely medieval vaulting high above them and let the calm dignity of those Gothic arches and vaults restore you!

Just inside the West Door you will see a portrait of King Richard II, son of the Black Prince, who succeeded his grandfather Edward III in 1377. The picture was painted a year or two after his accession, when he was in his early 'teens, and it is the earliest known portrait from life of an English king.

The Ambulatory

From the historical point of view the most interesting part of the Abbey is the east end, behind the high altar. Here is the shrine and chapel of Edward the Confessor, surrounded by a curved walkway or ambulatory—an unusual feature in an English church of this period. This ambulatory round the apse, with a number of small chapels opening off it, is a continental fashion which began to disappear in English church-building in the thirteenth century, giving way to the flat, chopped-off east end which you can see so clearly in Salisbury Cathedral, built at roughly the same time as Westminster. There is an admission fee of 2/- for the ambulatory.

The Confessor's Chapel

In the centre part of the apse is the shrine of St. Edward, surrounded by some of the early medieval kings and queens whom we have mentioned: Henry III, builder of the church, Edward I, the 'Hammer of the Scots' and his queen Eleanor, Richard II, whose portrait you saw earlier, Edward III and his plump and comfortable-looking Philippa. Here too is the Coronation Chair, built to house the Stone of Scone and used for every coronation in the Abbey from 1307 until now. East of the Confessor's shrine is the H-shaped chantry chapel of Henry V, the victor of Agincourt, his tomb beneath it and his funeral achievements—shield, helm, and saddle—on a beam above. You may wonder why Henry's effigy has no head. At the time of the Dissolution under Henry VIII when the monks of all closed religious orders were turned out of their monasteries, a great deal of looting went on, and it was then that Henry V's solid silver head, and the sheets of beaten silver which covered the oak core of the effigy, were stolen and have never been recovered. So poor King Henry has been headless for over four hundred years.

The Confessor's shrine in the centre of the chapel is sadly battered now, but you can still get an inkling of what it was like in its prime. It was encrusted with glass mosaic and precious stones, and must have glowed with colour. The style is curiously Eastern; in fact it was the work of Italian craftsmen, done in the Byzantine manner. The body of the saint is in the upper part of the shrine, above the arches placed there for pilgrims to kneel in and pray.

Splendid Perpendicular Gothic

Now move eastward past Henry V and you will come to a part of the Abbey which is about two hundred and fifty years later than the main church. Built by Henry VII, our first Tudor king, around 1500, it is a splendid example of the third and final phase of Gothic architecture. There are scores of examples of the style throughout England— Eton College chapel, King's College chapel at Cambridge, and St. George's chapel at Windsor among them —but Henry VII's chapel at Westminster is perhaps the most impressive, and certainly the most florid, of them all. Here you can see an example of that exclusively English development, fan vaulting, where the ribs of the pillars branch out at the top into beautiful curved conical shapes like the ribs of a fan. The vaulting of this chapel is not of plaster but of carved stone, fitted together into a very complex whole and held in place by keystones— they are the 'pendant' stones you see hanging downward from the vaulting, each one about 8 feet long and weighing a ton. Four and a half centuries ago this must have been a very daring feat of architecture.

Soon after the building of the Henry VII chapel, the Renaissance movement began to have its effect on architecture and design in England, and there is an interesting example here. The tomb of King Henry and his queen is in the new classical style, but the bronze screen around it is very obviously English Gothic.

The bones of Edward V and his younger brother

Richard—the 'Princes in the Tower'—are in a marble urn in the Queen Elizabeth chapel, which is really the north aisle of the Henry VII building.

Detail of a typical example of medieval carving

Chaucer's Tomb

Returning to the main church, turn now into the South Transept. This is often called 'Poets' Corner' from the number of poets, authors, playwrights and other men of letters who are either buried or commemorated there. Our main concern is with the medieval period, so we make our way half-way down the eastern side of the transept to a small tomb in the wall with a Gothic canopy. This is the burial place of Geoffrey Chaucer, author of *The Canterbury Tales* and probably the first poet to be buried in this part of the Abbey. It must be said, however, that the reason for his interment here was probably that he was Clerk of the King's Works for a time and spent the last years of his life in a house in the monastery garden nearby.

Cloister and Chapter House

Now you should go back to the aisle on the south side of the choir and through a door there into the cloister. This was a long time building, having been started in the mid-13th century and completed in the late 14th century. In the south walk of the cloister is a big tombstone under which are said to lie the twenty-six monks of Westminster who died of the Black Death in 1349. The arcading of the cloister was once glazed to keep out the wind and weather, for the medieval monks spent a lot of their time here, studying, working at their manuscripts, and so on. There would be rushes strewn on the pavement and lamps hung from the vaulting.

In the east cloister the Abbot used to hold his Maundy ceremony in Holy Week each year. Thirteen old men would be seated on the stone bench along the wall and the Abbot would wash their feet—which doubtless had already had the worst taken off!—and then kiss them, giving each man afterwards threepence, seven herrings, three loaves, and some ale.

The Chapter House, entered from the east walk of the cloister, is where the Abbot and his monks conducted the day-to-day administration of the monastery. It was also used for a time by the knights and burgesses summoned to Parliament, forerunners of the House of Commons. You will have to put on overshoes to go into the Chapter House, since it has a precious 13th-century tiled floor. The admission fee is 6d.

Outside the Abbey

Continuing your medieval Westminster walk outside the church, you should now leave by the small door near Chaucer's tomb in the south transept. The pathway outside offers you visual evidence of the development of Gothic architecture; the main part of the church and the chapter house, both in the plain and simple early English style of the 13th century, making a striking contrast with the outside of the Henry VII chapel, built in the highly decorative and elaborate style of about 1500—the Perpendicular. Here is a clear example of the distance covered by the Gothic builders in the space of two hundred and fifty years.

On the wall outside the south transept door is a tablet commemorating the fact that Caxton set up his printing press nearby in 1476.

The Jewel Tower

Across the road in front of you are the Houses of Parliament, or to use the official name, the Palace of Westminster. You will see that this impressive building echoes the Perpendicular style of Henry VII's chapel—but it is not genuine medieval architecture, having been built only in the 19th century.

Turn right past the statue of King George V and the handsome 18th-century houses facing up the street, and you will find the Jewel Tower on your right. This is one of the few relics of the medieval Palace of Westminster, most of which was destroyed in a disastrous fire in 1834. The Tower, probably built for Richard II about 1365, is a splendid example of Gothic domestic architecture— which was not in fact so very different from the church architecture of the period. It was so used for some time as a treasury for the crown jewels and later housed the official archives of Parliament. Now it is open to the public and well worth a visit.

The Burghers of Calais

Across the road, south of the great square Victoria Tower, is a public garden, and here you can see a replica of Rodin's famous group, *The Burghers of Calais*. The story is to be found in the summary of King Edward III's reign.

The road alongside the garden is called Millbank, and recalls the fact that the abbot of Westminster once owned a watermill nearby.

(Details of opening times, etc., of places mentioned above will be found in the Appendix.)

A Walk round Guildhall

Guildhall, centre of the City of London's government
and scene of treason trials, Lord Mayor's banquets, and
election of the City's officers, has been devastated twice
by fire, in 1666 and 1940. But the medieval crypt, porch,
and walls survived. The crypt is the earliest part of the
building and was begun in 1411. The great hall was
completed by 1440.

The Porch

Most of the interior of the porch is medieval, though the
outside has been restored from time to time. The oak
main doors are comparatively modern too.

The Walls and Roof

The walls are medieval and the hall measures 152 feet
by 49½ feet. High up you can see a frieze bearing the
coats of arms of England, the City of London, and the
twelve 'great' livery companies. The banners are those of
these twelve companies too. The roof of stone arches and
oak panelling is modern, replacing that destroyed in the
Blitz of 1940. The coats of arms you see up here are
those of all 82 livery companies.

The Windows

Turn left from the door and set in the south wall you will
see a window surviving from the 15th century, with some
horn panes instead of glass. The other windows are
modern, and carry the names of the mayors and Lord
Mayors of London—about 640 of them! The earliest are
in the west window above the gallery.

Gog and Magog

These two legendary giants are mentioned in the Old
Testament, and the medieval forerunners of the present
pair of figures were carried in the City's pageants for
centuries, being made of wickerwork. An 18th-century
pair were destroyed in 1940. Gog is on the right and
Magog on the left as you face the gallery.

In medieval and Elizabethan days Gog and Magog
were known as Gogmagog and Corineus, and legend had
it that they represented the conflict between the ancient
inhabitants of Britain and invaders from Troy a thousand
years before Christ, which resulted in the building here
of New Troy, capital of Albion! (If you happen to visit
Totnes in Devon during your holiday you may see the
'Brutus Stone' near the east gate of that town, which
popular legend would have us believe marks the spot
where Brutus, King of Troy, landed when he invaded
Albion.)

Monuments

Leaving the two giants and walking along the north wall
of the hall, you will come upon a fine statue of Sir
Winston Churchill by Oscar Nemon, then a monument to
Admiral Nelson. The gallery facing the main door is for
the press and television. Next comes a memorial to the
Duke of Wellington, then the Lady Mayoress's Gallery.
Another monument to William Pitt, Earl of Chatham, a
great 18th-century Prime Minister, and we have arrived at

the dais in the eastern end of the hall. This is where the Lord Mayor and Aldermen sit during meetings of the Court of Common Council and other municipal functions.

Returning along the south wall, we find first a memorial to the younger William Pitt, second son of the Earl of Chatham. This Pitt became Prime Minister in his twenty-fifth year, and was in office during much of the Napoleonic War period. Next to him is Lord Mayor Beckford; he is shown addressing a 'remonstrance' to George III, who had returned a terse and unfavourable reply to an address from the City complaining of a false return having been made in the Middlesex election of 1770.

Next is the oak canopy and buffet, in front of which the Lord Mayor and his principal guests sit at the annual banquet. And so we come back to the main door.

Guildhall's Surroundings

A great deal of new building has gone on around Guildhall to replace the bomb damage of the Second World War. Here and there, however, in the Gresham Street/Wood Street/Oat Lane area you can see some interesting relics of medieval times—small metal plaques bearing the coats of arms of the livery companies which own the property in this district, mainly the Goldsmiths and the Haberdashers. They are reminiscent of those old fire company insurance marks with which we are all familiar.

(Details of opening times, etc., are in Appendix.)

A Walk round the Tower of London

'Her Majesty's Palace and Fortress of the Tower of London' is of course one of the biggest and best-known of London's medieval buildings. Although no king or queen has lived there for over three hundred years, although it plays no military role in these nuclear days, and although there are no involuntary residents in its dungeons these days, the Tower still houses a community and still has a part to play as the repository of the Crown Jewels.

There is no reason why it should not be used again for the detention of state prisoners, should the need arise. After all, it is less than thirty years since the last such malefactor was made welcome—if that's the word; Rudolf Hess was held here for a short time after his flight to Britain in 1940. But we are concerned here with its medieval aspects.

The Tower of London is a so-called 'concentric' castle (see the chapter on medieval castles) but retains its early Norman keep in the centre. The outer and inner walls form an irregular pentagon and are surrounded by a wide moat, now drained.

Having bought your entrance tickets at the booths on the left as you go down the hill, you pass through the iron fence, and on your left is the site of the original outer gate, part of Lion Tower and built in the 13th century. You can still see the pit for the drawbridge, and the slots for its counterweights, which crossed the outer moat (now filled in). The Lion Tower was a big semi-circular building where the refreshment room now stands.

Now you bear left for the Middle Tower, outside which was a second drawbridge. Middle Tower was also built in the 13th century by Edward I, but has been refaced. Beyond the Middle Tower you walk along a causeway where there was once yet another drawbridge spanning the inner moat. This moat was drained in 1843 and is now sometimes used as a parade ground.

Next we come to the Byward Tower, part 13th and part 14th century. Beyond it we are between the inner and outer ring of walls, in the outer ward or bailey, which in this case is much narrower than in some other castles. On the left, forming the corner of the inner wall, is the Bell Tower. You can see the small belfry housing the curfew bell perched on top. This tower was probably planned about 1190, but it seems to date from a little later. Sir Thomas More, Bishop Fisher and Princess Elizabeth were imprisoned here in the 16th century.

Next we come to St. Thomas' Tower on the right, with the watergate beneath. Known as Traitors' Gate, since most important prisoners were brought to the Tower by boat, this is perhaps the most famous entrance to the fortress. One story says that the tower was originally dedicated to St. George, but after it had collapsed once or twice it was decided to rededicate it to St. Thomas Becket. He must be a more potent saint than George, as the tower has stayed intact since then.

Opposite Traitors' Gate is the entrance to the inner ward, the gateway built by Henry III in the thirteenth century, the upper part added about 1380. Originally known as the Garden Tower, it acquired its present name of Bloody Tower as early as 1597, being believed to have been the scene of the murder of Edward V and his brother.

Go through the arch, but before you turn left and up the steps to Bloody Tower, turn and look at the remains of the wall on your right. This was built by Henry III and formed the western side of the inmost bailey, the entrance to which was at the end of the ruined wall, through Coldharbour Tower, of which only the foundations remain. Henry III's wall and the remains of Coldharbour Tower were for a long time incorporated in a 19th-century building for the detachment of guardsmen quartered here. In December 1940 the Main Guard was destroyed by bombs and Henry's wall stood revealed again.

Bloody Tower

Now turn left through the small archway, up the steps and into Bloody Tower. The lower level was the prison of Sir Walter Raleigh for twelve years, and the furniture is approximately the type which would have been allowed to a distinguished prisoner. The two 'Princes in the Tower' were housed in the upper room, but the floor has now disappeared. In Bloody Tower there is also the windlass of the portcullis underneath, one of the few remaining in working order in England.

Tower Green

As you come out of Bloody Tower again you will see facing you Tower Green, and here, over towards the chapel on the far side, is the famous execution site. Although this scaffold site is so well known, it was in fact used only six times in all, being reserved for high-class personages like Anne Boleyn, Katherine Howard, and Lady Jane Grey. The more common execution place was outside the Tower (close to the modern Merchant Navy memorial on Tower Hill) where seventy-five people were beheaded.

Beauchamp Tower

Over to the left is Beauchamp Tower, built into the inner walls and originally entirely defensive in character. It was, however, often used as a prison for important persons, and is worth a visit to see the many inscriptions carved by inmates—though these mostly date from the 16th century and are not medieval.

The White Tower

This is the central keep of the fortress and the oldest part. Though of Norman construction and not medieval it was in use as a royal residence during the Middle Ages and saw a great deal of England's history in the making. The White Tower was held in pledge for the completion of Magna Carta in 1215 and 1216. During the wars with France, King David of Scotland, King John of France, Charles of Blois, and many other distinguished captives were held here. In 1399 King Richard II signed his abdication document in the White Tower and the Duke of Orleans, taken by Henry V at the Battle of Agincourt, was lodged here.

The White Tower now houses one of the finest collections of arms and armour in the world but unfortunately there is very little dated earlier than the 16th century and so it has almost nothing medieval to show.

The Crown Jewels

The Crown Jewels are now housed in a new Jewel House underneath the barrack block to the north of the White Tower. The entrance is at the western (left-hand) end of the block near Tower Green. Most of the regalia date from the restoration of Charles II in 1660 or later but there are some medieval survivals among them. Set in the front of the Crown of State is a huge uncut ruby which was given to Edward the Black Prince by King Pedro of Castile. There is a legend that this gem was worn in a gold circlet round his helm by Henry V at the

Battle of Agincourt. The other medieval pieces among the jewels are the Ampulla, a gold vessel in the form of an eagle in which is held the consecrated oil for the annointing of the Sovereign at the Coronation and the annointing spoon. The rest of the regalia is more recent.

You will not of course want to visit the Tower of London solely for its *medieval* connections; but since the earlier and later features will be described in other books in this series they have been omitted here.

(For opening times, etc., see Appendix A.)

APPENDIX A:
How to get there
London and Environs
CHARTERHOUSE
Charterhouse Square E.C.1. (off Aldersgate).
Admission 4s. 9d.
Open Wednesdays April to July only at 2.45 pm. Other times by appointment.
By Underground:
Aldersgate (Circle & Metropolitan lines).
By Car:
By Charterhouse Street, either from Aldersgate or Farringdon Road. Parking is difficult on weekdays.
ByBus:
4A, 141 to Aldersgate Underground.
7, 8, 22, 23, 25 to Giltspur Street.

CITY INFORMATION CENTRE
St. Paul's Churchyard (South side of Cathedral).
Telephone: MONarch 3030.

CROSBY HALL
Cheyne Walk, Chelsea, S.W.3. (Corner of Danvers Street).
Admission free.
Open weekdays 10—12 and 2—5. Saturdays and Sundays 2—5.
By Bus:
Routes 19, 39, 45, and 49 to Battersea Bridge.
By Car:
By Chelsea Embankment, Battersea Bridge, or Beaufort Street.

ELTHAM PALACE
King John's Walk, S.E.9 (Eltham High Street ½ mile).
Admission free.
Open Thursday and Sunday, summer 11 am—7pm, winter 11 am—4 pm.
By Bus:
Routes 21, 61, 89, 124, 160, 182, 228.
Green Line 717.

By Car:
By Eltham Hill or Eltham High Street (East-West);
South from Shooters Hill and Woolwich Common by
Well Hall Road.

GUILDHALL
Off Gresham Street, E.C.2.
Admission free: Open weekdays 10 am—5 pm. May to
September Sundays 2 pm—5 pm.
By Underground:
St. Paul's (Central line) or Bank (Central & Northern
lines) stations.
By Bus:
7, 8, 22, 23, 25 to King Street (Cheapside).
21, 43, 76 to Gresham Street.
By Car:
From Royal Exchange turn right along Princes Street,
left along Gresham Street, and right into Guildhall Yard.
Parking is difficult except at weekends out of 'meter
hours'.

LOMBARD STREET
E.C.3.
Approached from King William Street or Gracechurch
Street.
By Underground:
Bank (Central & Northern lines) or Monument (Circle &
District lines) stations.
By Bus:
7, 8, 22, 23, 25 to Royal Exchange.
35, 47 to Lombard Street.

OLD CURIOSITY SHOP
Portsmouth Street, W.C.2.
Open every day (including Sundays) 9.30 am—5.30 pm.
By Underground:
Holborn (Kingsway) station (Piccadilly & Central lines);
Aldwych station when open.
By Bus:
68, 77, 170, 188, 196 to Kingsway.
1, 6, 9, 11, 15 to Aldwych.

By Car:
Travelling south on Kingsway—turn left into Sardinia Street. Portsmouth Street is first right.
Travelling from east or west—drive round Aldwych one-way system past bottom of Kingsway, then first left into Houghton Street.

PRINCE HENRY'S ROOM
17 Fleet Street, E.C.4.
Open Monday to Friday 1.45—5 pm, Saturday 1.45—4.30 pm.
By Underground:
Temple station (Victoria Embankment) (District and Circle lines).
By Bus:
9, 11, 13, 15 to Temple Bar.
By Car:
From east or west along Victoria Embankment, turn 'inland' into Temple Place, then up Norfolk Street towards Strand. Metered area.

THE PRINTER'S DEVIL
New Fetter Lane, E.C.4.
Open during normal 'permitted hours' for City pubs.
By Underground:
Chancery Lane station (Central line).
By Bus:
171 to Chancery Lane or Fetter Lane.
9, 11, 13, 15 to Fetter Lane.
7, 8, 22, 23, 25 to Holborn Circus.
By Car:
Turn north into Fetter Lane from Fleet Street; or south down New Fetter Lane from Holborn Circus. Metered area.

PUDDING LANE
Runs south from Eastcheap to Lower Thames Street.
By Underground:
Monument station (Circle & District lines).
By Bus:
7, 8, 10, 21, 40, 44, 47 to North end of London Bridge.

By Car:
By Cannon Street (from the west) Great Tower Street and Eastcheap—or Lower Thames Street (from the east), and by Gracechurch Street (from the north).

RUNNYMEDE
On A.308 between Staines (one mile) and Windsor (three miles).
By Rail:
To Egham (Southern Region).
By Bus:
Green Line. 701, 702, 718, 725.
London Transport country bus route 441 from Windsor to Staines.

ST. BARTHOLOMEW-THE-GREAT
See Charterhouse.

ST. ETHELBURGA
Bishopsgate, E.C.2.
By Underground:
Liverpool Street (Circle, Central & Metropolitan lines).
By Bus:
6, 8, 22, 35, 47, 78, 149.

ST. ETHELDREDA
Ely Place, E.C.1. Off Charterhouse Street close to Holborn Circus.
By Underground:
Chancery Lane (Central line, closed Sundays).
By Bus:
7, 8, 22, 23, 25 to Holborn Circus.
17, 45, 221 to Charterhouse Street or Holborn Circus.
By Car:
From the north—by Farringdon Road (turn right at Charterhouse Street).
From the west—by Holborn (fork left at Holborn Circus).
From the east—by Newgate Street and Holborn Viaduct to Holborn Circus.

ST. HELEN'S
St. Helen's Place, Bishopsgate, E.C.1.

By Underground:
Liverpool Street (Circle, Central & Metropolitan lines).
By Bus:
As for St. Ethelburga's.

ST. MARY LE BOW
Cheapside, E.C.2.
By Underground:
St. Paul's (Central) or Bank (Central & Northern lines).
By Bus:
7, 8, 22, 23, 25 to Cheapside.

SOUTHWARK
(Cathedral, Site of Tabard Inn, etc.) South end of London Bridge.
By Underground:
London Bridge station (Northern line).
By Bus:
7, 8, 10, 13, 21, 35, 44, 47 to London Bridge (south end).
By Car:
From the north—over London Bridge.
From the west—by Southwark Street.
From the south—by Elephant & Castle and Borough High Street.
From the east—by Tooley Street.

STAPLE INN
Holborn, E.C.1.
By Underground:
By Bus:
See St. Etheldreda.

THE TEMPLE
E.C.4, between Fleet Street and Victoria Embankment.
By Underground:
Temple station (Circle & District lines, closed Sundays).
By Bus:
See Prince Henry's Room.
By Car:
   —ditto—

TOWER OF LONDON
E.C.3.
Admission 2/- (children 1/-).

116

Open weekdays May to September 10 am—5 pm;
October to mid-March 10 am—4 pm, mid-March & April
10 am—4.30 pm.
Sundays, Mid-March to October 2—5 pm.
By Underground:
Tower Hill station (Circle & District lines).
By Bus:
42, 78.
By Car:
From the west—by Great Tower Street or Lower
Thames Street.
From the east—by Commercial Road and Aldgate High
Street, then left into Minories.
From the south—by Tower Bridge.
From the north—by Bishopsgate, then left into Hounds-
ditch and Minories.
Car park under new building across road from Tower
(entrance from Lower Thames Street).

TYBURN
Site of public hanging gallows at junction of Edgware
Road and Oxford Street (near Marble Arch). A stone set
into the pedestrian 'island' at the junction marks the spot.
By Underground:
Marble Arch (**Central line**).
By Bus:
2, 6, 7, 8, 12, 15, 16, 36, 73, 74, 88 to Marble Arch.
By Car:
By Edgware Road from the north, Oxford Street from
the east, Park Lane from the south, and Bayswater Road
from the west.
Parking difficult when shops are open.

WEST SMITHFIELD
For St. Bartholomew-the-Great, Charterhouse Square, St.
Bartholomew's Hospital, St. John's priory.
By Underground:
Aldersgate (Circle & Metropolitan lines, closed Sundays)
or St. Paul's (Central line).
By Bus:
See Charterhouse.

By Car:
Turn out of Aldersgate Street into Long Lane, or from
Farringdon Road into Charterhouse Street (other side of
meat market).
Parking difficult on weekdays. At night beware big
lorries delivering meat to market.

WESTMINSTER
Abbey, Westminster Hall, Jewel Tower, St. Margaret's.
Westminster Abbey
Admission free to nave, transepts, cloisters. 2/- to ambu-
latory and royal chapels.
Open daily 8 am—6 pm (summer 7 pm); royal chapels
from 9.45 am (Tuesday and Friday 10.45 to 4 pm).
Westminster Hall
Admission free.
Open Monday to Friday 10 am—1.30 pm, Saturday
10 am—4 pm.
Jewel Tower
Admission free.
Open weekdays, (*Not* Wednesdays) March to September
10.30 am—6.30 pm.
October to February 10.30 am—4 pm.
By Underground:
Westminster or St. James' Park stations (Circle & District
lines).
By Bus:
3, 11, 12, 24, 59, 77, 88, 127, 134, 159 to Parliament Street.
By Car:
South down Whitehall to Parliament Square; from the
west along Chelsea Embankment and Millbank; from the
east along Victoria Embankment from the City, and turn
right at Big Ben; from the south via Westminster Bridge.
Metered area as far south as Horseferry Road. Parking
difficult except at weekends.

WINDSOR AND ETON
By M.4 turning left at Langley (just short of Slough) for
Windsor via Datchet. Thence through Eton.
Via Staines and Runnymede by A.308.

Castle:

> Admission to precincts free.
> State Apartments 2/- (child 6d).
> St. George's Chapel 2/- (child 1/-).

Times of opening and closing of State Apartments vary according to season, but normally 11 am to 3, 4 or 5 pm on weekdays; from 1.30 pm on Sundays (May to October only).

St. George's chapel, weekdays 11 am to 3.45 pm (Fridays from 1 pm), Sundays 2.30 to 4 pm.

By Rail:
Southern Region (about 45 minutes from Waterloo).

By Bus:
Green Line via Victoria—704, 705 (Express), 718.
725 from Gravesend, Croydon, etc., via Staines.

More Distant Places

ARUNDEL (Sussex)
60 miles south of London by A.24 and A.29; Arundel is 20 miles west of Brighton on A.27.
Castle with 'shell keep'.
Mid-April to June 20, Mons—Thurs, 1 to 4.30. June to September, Mons—Fris.
Admission 3/- (child 1/6).

BERKELEY (Glos.)
115 miles west of London, and about midway between Bristol and Gloucester, off A.38.
Another shell keep.
April—September, daily (not Mondays) 2 to 5.30 pm. 4/- (child 2/-).

BODIAM (Sussex)
55 miles south-east of London, a mile or two off A.268 between Hawkhurst and Northiam.
A small keep-less castle.
All year, weekdays 10 am to 7 pm (to sunset, October—March); April—September, Sundays 10 am to 7 pm.
Admission 1/6.

CAMBRIDGE
55 miles north of London by A.10.
College halls are a survival of medieval communal living.

CANTERBURY (Kent)
60 miles east-south-east of London by A.2. Cathedral—tombs of Henry IV and the Black Prince, place of Becket's martyrdom.
St. Thomas' Hospital—hospital for poor pilgrims.

COLCHESTER (Essex)
55 miles north-east of London by A.12. Castle is downhill from town centre past Town Hall.
Fine Norman castle keep, with important Roman museum. Open weekdays 10 am—5 pm, Sundays (April to Sept only) 2.30—5 pm. Admission free (Sundays 2/-).

GLOUCESTER
105 miles west-north-west of London by A.40.
Splendid Perpendicular Cathedral, tomb of Edward II.

HEDINGHAM (Essex)
50 miles north-east of London, and about 5 miles north of Halstead, just off A.604.
Huge Norman keep.
Open May—September: Tues, Thur, Sat, 2 to 6 pm.
Bank Holiday Mon, 10 am to 6 pm.
Admission 2/- (child 1/-).

HEVER (Kent)
30 miles south-south-east of London, 2 miles east of Edenbridge.
Fortified manor house.
Open Easter—September: Wednesdays, Sundays, and Bank Holidays, also Saturdays in August and September, 2—7 pm.
Admission 5/- (child 2/-).

ROCHESTER (Kent)
30 miles east of London by A.2.
120-foot-high Norman keep.

All year, weekdays 9.30 am to 7 pm (earlier in winter).
Admission 1/6 (child 9d.).

SOUTHWELL (Notts)
135 miles north of London, 7 miles west of Newark on
A.612.
Southwell Minster is famous for its naturalistic carving
(13th century). Some Norman work, and also has
examples of all three Gothic periods.

STOKESAY CASTLE (Salop)
150 miles north-west of London, on A.49 between
Ludlow and Craven Arms.
Probably Britain's best example of a fortified manor
house.
Open daily (not Tuesday), Summer 9 am to 6 pm, Winter
9 am to dusk.
Admission 3/- (child 1/-).

THETFORD (Norfolk)
85 miles north-east of London on A.11.
Biggest Norman castle motte in England. Turn right into
King Street and Castle Street, and castle mound is to the
right.

WALTHAM CROSS (Herts)
16 miles north of London, by A.10.
Has one of the three surviving Eleanor Crosses.
Trains from Liverpool Street, Green Line coaches (715)
from Oxford Circus.

WARWICK
90 miles north-west of London by A.41.
A fine keep-less castle (14th century).
Open weekdays, April to mid-October, 10 am to 5.30 pm;
October to March 10.30 am to 4 pm. Sundays (April—
October) 1 to 5 pm. Admission 5/- (child 2/6).

WORCESTER
115 miles north-west of London.
King John's tomb in the cathedral.

Appendix B : Museum List

London Museum

Address :   Kensington Palace,
                     Kensington Gardens, W.8
Admission :   Free
Opening hours :   1 March—30 September :
                     10 am—6 pm (Sundays : 2 pm—6 pm)
                     1 October—28 February :
                     10 am—4 pm (Sundays : 2 pm—4 pm)
Closed :   Good Friday, Christmas Eve, and
                     Christmas Day

Access :

By Underground :
Queensway (Central Line)—cross Bayswater Road and
walk through Broad Walk in Kensington Gardens to
Palace.
Kensington High Street (Circle & District Line from
Earls Court to Edgware Road)—turn right along Kensington High Street to Park. Left through Park to Palace.
By Bus :
12, 88, along Bayswater Road to Queensway, then as
above from Queensway Station.
9, 46, 52, 73, to Palace Gate in Kensington Road. Walk
through Park to Palace.

By Car:

The best place to park is in the squares and side streets off Bayswater Road or Kensington Road. Then walk through Park.

British Museum

Address: Great Russell Street, W.C.1
Admission: Free
Opening hours: Monday—Saturday: 10 am—5 pm
                      Sunday: 2.30 pm—6 pm
Closed: Christmas Day and Good Friday.
                      Open Bank Holidays usual hours
Access:

By Underground:

Tottenham Court Road (Central & Northern Lines)—turn right along Tottenham Court Road and right at Great Russell Street. Museum on left.

Russell Square (Piccadilly Line)—left out of station, cross Russell Square and left on Montague Street to Great Russell Street and main entrance of Museum.

By Bus:

77, 68, 188, 196, to Southampton Row. Turn left along Great Russell Street.

73 to Tottenham Court Road/Oxford Street. Right along Great Russell Street.

7, 8, 23, 25, to Bloomsbury Way. Turn along Museum Street (from West).

7, 8, 22, 23, 25, from Holborn direction. Alight at High Holborn, just past Kingsway, and cross road, along Drury Lane or Grape Street, cross New Oxford Street and continue along Coptic Street or Museum Street.

By Car:

Drive from West along Oxford Street, turn left at Tottenham Court Road and right almost immediately at Great Russell Street.

From East, along Holborn to Kingsway, turn right along Southampton Row and left at Great Russell Street.

N.B. There is limited parking at the Museum—otherwise,

at side in Montague Street/Russell Square.

Guildhall Museum

Address: On Bassishaw High Walk, up stairs by
                  Gillette House in Basinghall Street,
                  overlooking London Wall, E.C.2
Admission: Free
Opening hours: Monday—Saturday: 10 am—5 pm
Closed: Sundays, Bank Holidays, Holy Days—
                  e.g. Christmas and Good Friday
Access:

By Underground:
Aldersgate (Metropolitan or Circle Lines)—turn right out
of station along Aldersgate as far as London Wall. Turn
left—Museum up on high walk-way opposite ruin of
church tower.
St. Paul's (Central Line)—walk along Cheapside to Wood
Street, left to Gresham Street, right for one block to
Aldermanbury. Up stairs on right at end before junction
with London Wall.
By Underground:
Moorgate (Metropolitan & Northern Lines)—turn right
along Moorgate, to London Wall. Turn right.
Bank (Central Line)—along Princes Street at side of
Bank of England to Gresham Street. Left as far as
Basinghall Street. Right. Museum at far end of Basing-
hall Street up steps by Gillette House.
By Bus:
7, 8, 22, 23, 25, to St. Paul's end of Cheapside, then
follow instructions given under St. Paul's Underground
Station above.
76, 43, 21, 11, 9, 141, to London Wall/Moorgate. Follow
instructions as from Moorgate Station.
By Car:
Parking is difficult except at weekends out of 'meter'
hours. No parking at any time on London Wall.
From East: drive to the Bank then along Princes Street

124

by Bank of England, turn left at Gresham Street and right at Aldermanbury.

From West: Holborn/Newgate Street, turn left at Aldersgate and right at Gresham Street. Park in area behind Guildhall.

Further reading list

J. J. Bagley — *Life in Medieval England,* Batsford

W. O. Hassall — *They Saw It Happen,* Basil Blackwell

R. J. Mitchell & M. D. R. Leys — *A History of London Life,* Penguin Books

H. V. Morton — *In Search of London,* Methuen

E. Rickert (compiled by), C. C. Oson & M. M. Crow (edited by) — *Chaucer's World,* Oxford University Press

John Stow (Although Stow was a 16th-century chronicler, he had much to say about medieval times.) — *Survey of London*

A large number of leaflets, including the Official Guide to the City of London, published by the Corporation of the City, are available from the City Information Centre, St. Paul's Churchyard.

The 'Pride of Britain' series, published by Pitkin Pictorials, include many dealing with buildings and events in the City of London.